The Pawnee

Titles in the Indigenous Peoples of North America Series Include:

The Pawnee

Stuart A. Kallen

Lucent Books, Inc.
P.O. Box 289011, San Diego, California

Library of Congress Cataloging-in-Publication Data

Kallen, Stuart A., 1955–
  The Pawnee / by Stuart A. Kallen.
    p. cm. — (Indigenous peoples of North America)
Includes bibliographical references and index.
  ISBN 1-56006-825-6 (hardback : alk. paper)
  1. Pawnee Indians—History—Juvenile literature. 2. Pawnee Indians—
Social life and customs—Juvenile literature. [1. Pawnee Indians. 2. Indians
of North America—Great Plains.] I. Title. II. Series.
  E99.P3 K36 2001
  978'.004979—dc21
                                              00-012365

Contents

Foreword

North America's native peoples are often relegated to history—viewed primarily as remnants of another era—or cast in the stereotypical images long found in popular entertainment and even literature. Efforts to characterize Native Americans typically result in idealized portrayals of spiritualists communing with nature or bigoted descriptions of savages incapable of living in civilized society. Lost in these unfortunate images is the rich variety of customs, beliefs, and values that comprised—and still comprise—many of North America's native populations.

The *Indigenous Peoples of North America* series strives to present a complex, realistic picture of the many and varied Native American cultures. Each book in the series offers historical perspectives as well as a view of contemporary life of individual tribes and tribes that share a common region. The series examines traditional family life, spirituality, interaction with other native and non-native peoples, warfare, and the ways the environment shaped the lives and cultures of North America's indigenous populations. Each book ends with a discussion of life today for the Native Americans of a given region or tribe.

In any discussion of the Native American experience, there are bound to be sim-

ilarities. All tribes share a past filled with unceasing white expansion and resistance that led to more than four hundred years of conflict. One U.S. administration after another pursued this goal and fought Indians who attempted to defend their homelands and ways of life. Although no war was ever formally declared, the U.S. policy of conquest precluded any chance of white and Native American peoples living together peacefully. Between 1780 and 1890, Americans killed hundreds of thousands of Indians and wiped out whole tribes.

The Indians lost the fight for their land and ways of life, though not for lack of bravery, skill, or a sense of purpose. They simply could not contend with the overwhelming numbers of whites arriving from Europe or the superior weapons they brought with them. Lack of unity also contributed to the defeat of the Native Americans. For most, tribal identity was more important than racial identity. This loyalty left the Indians at a distinct disadvantage. Whites had a strong racial identity and they fought alongside each other even when there was disagreement because they shared a racial destiny.

Although all Native Americans share this tragic history they have many distinct differences. For example, some tribes and individuals sought to cooperate almost immediately with the U.S. government while others steadfastly resisted the white presence. Life before the arrival of white settlers also varied. The nomads of the Plains developed altogether different lifestyles and customs from the fishermen of the Northwest coast.

Contemporary life is no different in this regard. Many Native Americans—forced onto reservations by the American government—struggle with poverty, poor health, and inferior schooling. But others have regained a sense of pride in themselves and their heritage, enabling them to search out new routes to self-sufficiency and prosperity.

The *Indigenous Peoples of North America* series attempts to capture the differences as well as similarities that make up the experiences of North America's native populations—both past and present. Fully documented primary and secondary source quotations enliven the text. Sidebars highlight events, personalities, and traditions. Bibliographies provide readers with ideas for further research. In all, each book in this dynamic series provides students with a wealth of information as well as launching points for further research.

The People of the Plains

The Great Plains of the United States is a vast expanse of flat, arid territory that stretches from the Mississippi River to the Rocky Mountains. For thousands of years this huge spread of rugged land was virtually deserted except for eagles, pronghorn antelope, elk, deer, wolf, coyote, jackrabbits, prairie dogs, and millions of American bison, or buffalo.

Around A.D. 1200, the Pawnee became one of the first tribes to settle the Great Plains. They came north from their ancestral home in Mississippi and east Texas near the Gulf of Mexico. These wanderers settled along the banks of the Loup, Platte, and Republican Rivers in present-day Nebraska. The region was well suited to survival with fertile soil, abundant game, and life-giving rivers and lakes.

The Pawnee of the plains were related to the Caddo who originally lived in Mexico. The Pawnee name is believed to have come from the Caddoan word *pariki*, which means horn, based on the male Pawnee custom of rubbing buffalo fat and paint in the

hair to make it stand erect like an animal's horn. The Pawnee called themselves *Chahiksichahiks*, meaning "men of men."

During their first centuries in the isolated Nebraska grasslands, the Pawnee had the land mostly to themselves. Without competition for resources or space, their numbers grew to more than thirty-five thousand. Gradually, the tribe separated into four bands, each living independent of the others but sharing a common heritage.

The *Chaui,* or Grand, lived near the Platte in Nebraska and the Arkansas River in Kansas. They were neighbors to the *Pitahauerat*, or *Tappage*, tribe that lived in the same region. The *Kitkehahaki*, or Republican band, lived on the Republican River in Nebraska and the *Skidi*, or Wolf, tribe spread out across the flat prairie of northern Nebraska with villages on the north fork of the Loup River.

The tribal bands did not remain isolated for long. The abundance of food and water that attracted the Pawnee to the region also brought nomadic tribes from elsewhere. By the eighteenth century there were more than thirty-two tribes on the huge expanse of the Great Plains.

Although the Pawnee were Plains Indians, their way of life differed significantly from other tribes in the region. While most Plains tribes (such as the Cheyenne) were hunters, the Pawnee were an agricultural people. They settled in permanent villages and built lodges from earth, grass, and wood. They organized large-scale buffalo hunts twice a year and grew corn, beans, squash, and other crops.

A Rich Culture

The deeply spiritual Pawnee developed a rich culture over the centuries that included dozens of rituals and ceremonies based on planting and harvesting corn. They believed that their gods had given them the corn and the buffalo, and that the Pawnee themselves had descended directly from the moon, planets, and stars in the night sky.

With roots in both the spirit world and the fertile prairie soil the Pawnee lived in harmony with their natural surroundings. The people of the earth lodges were farmers, healers, warriors, astronomers, artists, storytellers, dancers, and more. Days were spent hunting and tending corn crops in the fields, nights were enlivened by religious rituals and ceremonial performances.

The Pawnee pursed their unique way of life for more than five hundred years until

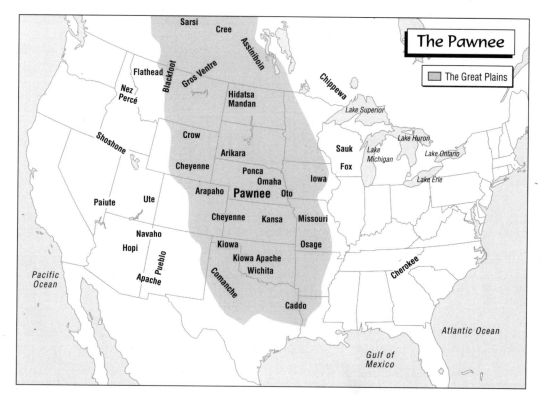

French and English explorers began to filter into the region in the late eighteenth century. The growing presence of these outsiders brought monumental change to the Pawnee earth lodge villages. For the next two hundred years, guns, horses, and European diseases weakened Pawnee power in the region. When their homeland was finally confiscated by the U.S. government in the nineteenth century, the ancient Pawnee way of life came to an abrupt end. In the subsequent years the people of the plains would find themselves struggling to maintain their identity and trying to survive as a united people in a hostile new world that was not of their making.

Chapter 1

Villages on the Plains

In the warm climate of east Texas, prior to their move to Nebraska, the Pawnee lived in circular lodges constructed from thatched grass. When they left their ancestral home in the thirteenth century, they wandered north more than three hundred miles until they found the sparsely populated region along the banks of the Loup River in southeastern Nebraska. There, they developed new skills that would help them survive in this environment, which was drastically different from their homeland.

The Earth Lodge

The Pawnee are defined as a semisedentary tribe, or people who live in one place for about half the year. They lived in tepees on their semiannual buffalo hunts, but their permanent shelters were called earth lodges.

The earth lodge was a dome-shaped home built over a framework of log poles that were covered with clumps of dirt and grass known as sod. Four to eight families lived in each lodge, and the ingenious design of these structures protected their in-habitants from searing heat, pouring rain, bone-chilling winds, and snow.

To build an earth lodge, men picked out a level area of terrain and drew a circle from twenty-five to sixty feet in diameter. The sod was removed from within this circle, and a hole was dug into the hard prairie soil to a depth of about one foot. The mud and sod were piled up in embankments at the edges of the circle.

Cottonwood logs about a foot thick and eight feet long were then planted upright about eight feet apart from one another along the edge of the circle. Each log had a Y-shaped notch at the top into which long connecting beams were laid. Smaller posts were planted in the outer edges of the circle and leaned in toward the center to form sloping outer walls.

Another circular framework of ten-foot-long logs was constructed toward the center of the lodge in order to hold up the roof. More poles were laid across the top of this framework and the beams of the entire structure were joined by poles and lashed

The Tepee

When the Pawnee traveled across the prairie during the winter in search of buffalo, they lived in tepees. Matthew W. Stirling describes the tepee in "Indians of Our Western Plains," an article in the July 1944 *National Geographic*:

"For the cover of a typical tepee, 10 or 12 buffalo skins were required. These were divested of hair and tanned on both sides, then skillfully tailored to fit tightly over the conical framework of poles. The tent poles were usually from 14 to 16 feet long. The bark was peeled off and the poles rubbed smooth.

A Pawnee tepee was considered the woman's property and responsibility.

To erect the frame, three or four poles . . . were laid on the ground and lashed together about three feet from the small ends. These tied poles, were raised and . . . firmly set in the ground.

Ten to 20 more poles, according to the size of the tent, were then arranged with their bases in a circle and the upper ends laid in the forks made by the tied ends of the original poles. These were set in place so they would lock one another, making a frame firm enough to resist a high wind.

A flap was built in the upper portion of the cover, next to the opening on top, for use as a ventilator. This was attached to a separate pole, the position of which could be changed according to the direction of the wind.

Making, erecting, and transporting the tepee was strictly the work of the woman, and the tepee was considered to be her property. Frequently it was decorated by painting.

A simpler, more graceful, or practical dwelling was never devised by man."

together with strips of bark. At the very center of the lodge, a hole about four feet across was left to later allow smoke from a central fire pit to escape. A center pit dug three to four feet in diameter served as a fireplace.

To finish, builders lashed willow branches together tightly across the top of the framework. This was topped by heavy grass thatch, woven so expertly that rainwater could not penetrate its construction. In other climates this might have been sufficient to protect the families within the earth lodge. But in Nebraska it was necessary to cover the willows with thick rectangular clumps of sod laid in overlapping patterns like shingles. The entire structure was then crowned with soil that was tamped down to make the earth lodge impervious to even the harshest prairie weather.

On the opening on the eastern wall—facing the sunrise—a long tunnel was constructed to act as a doorway. The inner and outer entrances of this vestibule were covered with thick buffalo skins to keep out wild animals and bad weather. Firewood was stored in piles along the walls of the tunnel.

A sunken room was constructed to store food. A description of it appears in a July 1944 *National Geographic* article by Matthew W. Stirling:

> Near the entrance of the earth lodge a sort of miniature cellar was built. This was a hole in the ground about 8 feet deep, rounded on the sides and bottom and with an opening just large enough to admit a person. It was lined with poles and grass and covered with sod.

> In this the winter food supply was placed, consisting mainly of corn and dried meat, carefully packed. The skins

While the Pawnee lived in tepees during buffalo hunts, they used earth lodges for permanent shelter during the rest of the year.

and extra clothing were as a rule also kept in the cache, to be out of the way.[1]

Inside the Lodge

After the lodge was constructed, builders turned their attention to the inside of the structure. The floor was formed by using human foot power to pack down the earth. Once tamped tight and level, the floor was flooded with water, drained, covered with dry grass, and set on fire. This process was often repeated several times until the floor was as hard and glazed as tile, and just as easy to keep clean.

The walls of the earth lodge were lined with couches—rectangular frame structures made from poles and covered with cozy piles of buffalo robes. People slept on the couches at night and used them as seats during the day. One couch might serve as a bed for an entire family of mother, father, and several children. Others might be used by only children, or a

Repairing and Rebuilding the Earth Lodge

The earth lodge sat vacant throughout the long winter, while its occupants traveled the prairies on the trail of the buffalo. During this time the shelter was often buried under a thick crust of ice and snow. Earth lodges lasted about fifteen years, and the shelter often had to be repaired—and eventually rebuilt. This process is described by Gene Weltfish in *The Lost Universe:*

"By spring, when the snow began to melt, the water seeping through the hard-packed earth and the thick layer of thatch might reach some of the radial timbers and rot them. Each household had to come to a decision as to whether to rebuild the whole house or just to mend the roof. This depended on the age of the house and the extent of the damage. They would count only on fifteen years as the maximum life of the house, and, when they anticipated a need for rebuilding

they had to plan at least two years in advance to locate, process, and season the timbers, grass, and other materials. A man who was influential in the community could count on extra help from his fellow villagers who would gladly volunteer, while a less important person had to depend on whatever labor force was available in the house itself. It took eighty-six to ninety man-woman days of labor to repair the roof of an earth lodge. It was a construction job that was accomplished with no overseer and no commands. A great deal of individual labor was consumed in preparing the materials, and this was done mainly by members of the household over a period of time. The actual construction work took only three days and was accomplished with a large number of volunteers. By way of compensation [for the work], the women of the household had to feed from thirty to fifty [workers] for at least three meals."

single elder. In *The Lost Universe*, anthropologist Gene Weltfish describes the built-in Pawnee couch:

The bedding was designed to keep the occupants warm and to ensure a certain amount of privacy. The basic bedclothes [were made from] two layers of tanned hide. At the head were skin pillows stuffed with turkey feathers or deer hair. Sometimes a roll of discarded [animal] skin clothing was used instead. At the foot was also a roll of worn out skin clothing against which one could rest one's feet. A skin curtain hung at the head and the foot of every bed, suspended from the roof for privacy. These were tucked in underneath before putting down the bedclothes to keep anything natural [such as mice] or supernatural [such as bad spirits] from coming into the bed at night. In the more luxuriously appointed beds, an extra skin curtain was suspended against the wall so that should any mice living in the thatch loosen any earth, it would fall behind the curtain. The curtains were usually made of discarded pieces of tanned buffalo-hide tent skin. When they went to bed, everyone disrobed. In the warmer weather they covered themselves with a tanned skin—preferably elk or deerskin. . . . This was commonly dyed black and was worn as a wraparound garment during the day.[2]

This nineteenth-century engraving depicts typical life in a Pawnee camp.

Some couches were used only for storage of household items. The western wall of the lodge was reserved for a sacred altar where religious ceremonies were performed under a mounted buffalo skull.

The fire pit in the middle of the earth lodge was a busy center of activity, for it was here that all meals were cooked and families gathered at night to gossip and tell stories. The smoke hole high above the fireplace let out wispy columns of smoke in the day, and let in a warming shaft of sun at dawn. As Stirling writes: "The earth lodge was airy, clean, and admirably suited to the . . . [weather] of the . . . Plains."[3]

Household Chores

Pawnee earth lodges buzzed with activity, housing as many as eight families—up to fifty men, women, and children—in each one. The residents of the lodges not only ate and slept there, but also used their

Gathering Firewood

The Nebraska plains have few forested areas to supply the necessary firewood required by the Pawnee. In *The Roots of Dependency*, Richard White writes about the wood shortages faced by the tribe:

"When they selected village sites in . . . river valleys, the Pawnees sought both fertile corn lands and available supplies of timber. But sufficient amounts of timber became hard to find, especially as the villages grew larger. . . . The Pawnees needed firewood for cooking, heating, making pottery, and drying corn. Cooking utensils and bowls came from black oak, post oak, and elm. Tipi poles, usually of cottonwood, required more timber, but the earthlodges represented the greatest drain of wood supplies. On the Republican [River] the Pawnees apparently used oak for building, while on the Platte and Loup [Rivers] they preferred elm but often had to resort to cottonwood, a tree poor in both strength and durability. . . . By the 1830s the Pawnees often got wood for the earthlodges at Grand Island and floated it downstream. By 1835 the demand for wood at [one] Skidi village . . . had so depleted the trees that women were forced to go seven or eight miles to secure firewood and timber to repair the lodges."

shelters for workshops and recreational centers.

Although there were many people to help with chores, daily life was filled with hard work. Cooking, carrying water, and finding firewood required great physical effort. For instance, water needed to be brought into the household at least twice a day. Women could often be seen walking to the nearest creek with two buckets hanging from long poles resting on their shoulders.

Much of the work inside the lodge was also performed by women. Weltfish explains:

There were two main meals a day . . . both serving all. In operation this meant that the woman who cooked the meal had raised all the vegetables in her own gardens, had dried and preserved them and kept them in her storage pit, and that all the meat she served was dried and packed by her on the buffalo hunt, carried back to the village (on her back or by the dogs she raised). . . . In the past, the clay pot she cooked in would have been made by her . . . and she [made] the large buffalo-horn ladle with which she served, the wooden mortar and pestle in which the mush was pounded, and . . . the wooden bowls and buffalo-horn spoons in which the food was served, the rush mats on which the people sat, and all the clothing they wore. Every day, morning or evening, she would serve twenty, thirty, forty, or fifty people a meal.[4]

To efficiently perform the daily tasks of feeding the families, women followed a hierarchy based on age. Mature women oversaw food supplies, picked recipes, and directed the work. Younger women and those newly married performed cooking and cleaning chores.

The oldest women of the household cared for the small children and were referred to as "grandmother" no matter what their actual biological relation to the children. Small children were fed by their "grandmothers" at mealtime and sometimes shared beds with them at night. The eldest women in the household also helped with the cooking.

With so many people living so close together along with all manner of stored food, vermin such as fleas, bedbugs, and mice could become a serious problem. The job of ridding the earth lodge of pests fell to the older women. Weltfish describes the process of fumigation:

The three old ladies met at the lodge in the morning. . . . They made a brush or short broom of dry *pakuts* (thatch) grass and tied it to a stick. Then each woman took her brush inside the lodge and lit the grass, each one going around one side of the room and being careful to stay near the floor as the dry grass in the roof

thatch might catch fire. When the grass was burned up on their broom, they put some more grass on it and repeated the process throughout the day. They repeated this four days later, and then on subsequent days. They built a little fire in the fireplace and burnt some wild sage . . . as incense to clear the air and make the room smell good. They would also burn some of the sage on their brooms along with the other grass. After the final smoking, they left the lodge empty for a day and on the following evening the lodge was quite habitable.[5]

Working with Wood

In addition to their household chores, Pawnee women were skilled woodworkers who produced almost all utensils found within an earth lodge. Trees were scarce on the Nebraska plains, growing only along riverbanks, and women often had to travel great distances to find suitable wood for their craft. Women carved mortar and pestles for grinding corn and herbs, wooden bowls and ladles for serving, and buffalo-horn spoons for eating.

Before eighteenth-century white settlers brought metal tools such as axes and files, wooden items had to be carved with sharp pieces of clamshell or bone. This was a painstaking task—it might take a woman eight days to carve a simple bowl from a wooden knot of cottonwood or oak. Even with metal tools, bowl carving could take up to three days.

In addition to managing all the chores of daily life, Pawnee women were skilled woodworkers and seamstresses. They made all of the tribe's utensils and clothing.

Effie Blane, a woman of the Pitahawirata Pawnee tribe, describes the bowl-making process:

> For a wooden bowl or *rakaraki*, one would select the knot [of wood] according to the size of the bowl one wanted. After the knot is cut with a sharp hatchet, the woman would begin to chip it from the middle out, and finally while the wood was still damp and not hard she would make a hole on the inner surface of the requisite size. Next she trimmed all over with a crooked knife, *retsi-pirus*, "knife-crooked," leaving a projection on the rim to be formed into a handle. When the surface was all smooth, she carved the handle called *rak-u-paks-tar-u-kita-ku*, "plate-with-head-plural-up-on top-sitting" the handle being toothed on top. After the carving was done, it was scraped and polished until it was a beautiful bowl. Then it was well greased. Several bowls were made at time. A bowl took at least three days to make.[6]

To make spoons, women always kept a supply of buffalo horns on hand. The horns were placed in the hot coals of the fire pit until they became soft and malleable and could be expanded by a woman pressing down on them with her foot. Blane explains:

"Then the small end was notched and scraped and the whole thing greased. When several were finished, holes were bored into the handles and they were strung on a buckskin string to be hung up when out of use."[7]

Women who made utensils for other members of the tribe were paid with various items. Fair payment for a bowl might include a bag of dried roasted corn kernels about six inches high or some deerskins that could be made into moccasins or leggings. For a large mortar and pestle, which could take up to five days of labor, a woman could earn five yards of calico cloth, a blanket, and some corn, or as one unnamed Pawnee said: "Something for the person to wear and something for the family to eat."[8]

Making Clothing

In addition to her other chores, a Pawnee woman made all the clothing worn by her family. For herself, she made dresses, wraparound skirts, blouses, and leggings from buckskin. For the men, a Pawnee seamstress

Carving Sacred Pipes

While women carved most household utensils, Pawnee men carved sacred pipes that were smoked at religious ceremonies, war councils, and other social gatherings.

The stem of the pipe was symbolic of the human throat and the smoke drawn through it was considered as sacred as air. A pipe stem was carved from a stick of ash about twenty inches long that had been gently heated over a fire and straightened. After the bark was peeled off the stick, the soft wood, or pith, in the center was burned out using the stem of a plant known as fuzzy weed. The stiff and sharp weed was used to burn the pith all the way down the stem and enlarge it once a small hole was made.

The bowl of the pipe was carved from the soft red pipestone (catlinite) that was quarried in southwestern Minnesota and traded in Native American communities throughout North America. Before the introduction of metal drills, files, and rasps, hollowing out and carving this stone required days of patient labor.

To hollow out the bowl of the pipe, men used a sharp sliver of buffalo bone, slowly scraping away minute particles of rock. This tedious process took a pipe maker up to eight eight-hour days. After the pipe was finished, the stem was decorated with brown, white, and black eagle feathers, each color holding a specific religious significance.

Men smoked mixtures of tobacco and herbs in their pipes. The Pawnee grew their own tobacco in their gardens, and it was considered a sacred plant that symbolized a "breath of life," which created a social bond between people.

made breechclouts (loincloths), buckskin shirts, and leggings. A Pawnee man also needed two belts to wrap around his waist. He used one to hold up his leggings, and the other to hang his knife, gun, pipe, pouch, and tomahawk. Children were dressed in similar outfits as their parents. Men, women, and children also wore long robes made from buffalo hide.

Pawnee ceremonial clothing was colorful and elaborately decorated.

In addition to these everyday clothes, a Pawnee family had special clothing for ceremonies, war, and hunting. Ceremonial clothing—and items worn by priests and chiefs—were decorated with porcupine quills, beads, feathers, and painted designs made from vegetable and mineral dyes. Ceremonial clothing might be made with buffalo or hides of beaver, raccoon, otter, elk, and deer.

The Pawnee, like all other Native American tribes, had their own unique moccasin designs. For daily wear, women constructed unadorned moccasins from two separately cut pieces of buffalo hide. Ceremonial moccasins were beaded and decorated with porcupine quills.

Moccasins worn in snow and rain were made from the tops of old tepees that had been immersed in wood smoke over the years. Thomas E. Mails explains the details of cold-weather moccasins in *The Mystic Warriors of the Plains:*

> Footwear made from [old tepees] was not perfectly waterproof, but they never became hard or cracked from continuous use during the wet season as unsmoked hides did, and furthermore, they dried smooth without stretching. Winter moccasins either were made with the hair turned in or else cut extra large so as to fit over heavy inner wrappings which were used on the feet [for warmth]. During the coldest seasons, buffalo hair, leaves, or sagebrush bark was matted into insulation pads of different thicknesses which the Indians wrapped

around their feet before donning their moccasins. Cold-weather moccasins were also made with high tops to protect the ankles, and with very long laces to wrap and tie them tightly about the ankle. Since they were designed only for service, they were seldom decorated in any way. In addition, the men sometimes put several applications of grease on the soles to make them more waterproof.[9]

Guests and Visitors

Pawnee women took great pride in their sewing skills and were eager to show off their finest moccasins when visitors came to call. Social gatherings were an important part of daily life in the earth lodge, but there were strict rules of etiquette that visitors were expected to follow when in another family's earth lodge.

When entering the earth lodge, men always walked in first followed by women. It was considered rude to walk between two people who were talking, and casual conversations were never held on the west side of the lodge, where the sacred altar stood.

Visitors to the earth lodge were always given the best seat in the house—a buffalo robe next to the fire pit. When guests arrived, they were expected to sit quietly for a few moments while the sacred pipe was smoked. A person's tribal status determined the order in which he or she spoke—a well-respected chief spoke first while a young warrior would patiently wait for the elder to begin the conversation.

After serious matters were discussed, women served food to everyone at the gathering. Guests were expected to eat everything offered them—refusing a helping of food was considered impolite. After important business was concluded, conversation turned to jokes, stories, and gossip. In *Pawnee Hero Stories and Folk Tales*, George Bird Grinnell writes of his experiences as a visitor to a nineteenth-century Pawnee village:

> In their personal [interaction] with each other, and with strangers, the Pawnees were kindly and accommodating. I have had [great] kindnesses . . . done me by Pawnee men, such as I should never expect to receive from white persons not [related to me]. In the village, the well-to-do gave freely to those who were poor, and all were very hospitable. They were a light-hearted, merry race, keenly alive to the ridiculous [aspects of life], and very fond of a joke. They were great chatterers, and had about them nothing of the supposed [seriousness] of the Indian. Of modesty or delicacy in conversation, as we know it, they had none. Both sexes spoke freely to each other of matters which are never mentioned in [white] society, and much of their conversation, as well as many of their [bawdy] stories, could not well be printed.[10]

The Village Community

The spirit of friendship and cooperation within each earth lodge was an extension of

Pawnee society was built on cooperation. Each person was expected to participate in the community and Pawnee chiefs did not act without the consensus of the tribe.

Pawnee society as a whole, and each village was made up of ten or twelve earth lodges whose residents worked together as a community. The villages themselves were aligned with specific bands of the Pawnee tribe.

The Skidi, for instance, were the most numerous of the four Pawnee subtribes. In the early 1700s they lived in about twenty separate villages, each with an estimated population of three hundred to five hundred. Their villages had names such as Village-in-the-Bottomlands (*Tuhitspiat*), Wolf-in-Water (Tskirirara), and Pumpkin-Vine (Pahukstatu).

Village life depended on each person performing his or her civic duties rather than on the dictates of one strong leader. Weltfish marveled at the smooth-running efficiency of the Pawnee community:

In all [their] work, both public and private, the Pawnee moved on a totally voluntary basis. . . . As I talked to the old men and women . . . [and] they described the coordination of their households, I repeatedly asked when they got together and [formed] the plan they were . . . carrying through and in what exact terms they discussed it. The answer was always, "They didn't discuss it at all. They don't talk about it. It goes along just as it happens to work out."

For example, sentinels were always needed to man the outposts and keep watch for the enemy who might be lurking nearby ready to attack the villages, or in the process of sneaking up on them. Sentinels were neither assigned nor called for by anyone. A number of young men who were friends would be talking together and one would mention that this was about the time the enemy would be attacking. Then one of them would remark, "I think I'll go up to the sentry post early tomorrow morning." Another would say, "I think I'll do that too." Then several others would chime in and word would get around, and other young men would also turn up long before dawn at the different sentry posts.[11]

The cooperation described by Weltfish was enhanced by tribal chiefs, who were chosen for their diplomacy and humility, rather than their aggressive temperaments. When important business needed to be conducted, chiefs used envoys to travel between lodges to discuss matters, gather opinions, and analyze problems. No leader would dare act without the consensus of the people, and if a chief tried to enforce an unpopular decision, he would simply be ignored.

With a relatively small population spread out across an isolated area, the Pawnee formed cooperative communities that were marvels of democracy and individual empowerment. While they relied on one another for survival, they were remarkably independent, extracting the necessities for daily life from the bounty of nature. In this spirit of harmony, the Pawnee successfully endured on the Nebraska prairie for more than five hundred years.

Chapter 2

The Circle of the Seasons

The Pawnee survived by hunting, farming, and gathering wild foods. They lived their lives according to the seasons and moved through the Nebraska plains in an ancient rhythm of existence. From April through June, they lived in earth-lodge villages and planted large gardens. During this time, they also made clothes, utensils, weapons, tepees, and other items necessary for daily life.

As the days grew longer and the hot sun of summer parched the plains, every villager who could walk or ride left home and headed west for the buffalo hunt conducted during the months of July and August. Throughout the summer the Pawnee lived in tepees in temporary villages strung out along the Platte and Republican Rivers. At the beginning of September, the Pawnee—heavily laden with dried buffalo meat, bones, and skins—returned to their earth lodges to harvest the crops. When produce was dried and stored, a thirty-day season of religious rituals, celebrations, and festivals began. Around November 15, when the icy

winds of winter began to blow across the prairie, the Pawnee once again loaded their tepees onto their horses and headed west for the winter buffalo hunt.

The Pawnee were unique among Plains tribes in that they maintained two separate residences, living in earth lodges five months of the year, while staying in tepees the rest of the year. They were tough people who survived with equal skill in the scorching Nebraska summer heat, drenching prairie downpours, and the icy January windchill. Their lives were dictated by the circular cadence of the seasons, and they lived in harmony with the best and the worst that nature had to offer.

Spring Planting

Pawnee women were skilled farmers who began the agricultural year in early April, when the spring rains had washed away the last of the snow. The first job was to clear debris from the fields, a task in which women were helped by men and children. Roots and rocks were removed, weeds were pulled, and the stubble from the previous year's crops was burned.

During planting time, women used hoes made from buffalo shoulder blades. Seeds were planted in corn hills about two feet high and eighteen inches in diameter. Each mound was planted with five to seven seeds and lightly patted down into a smooth hill. Native Americans grew many varieties of corn, and the Pawnee planted white, blue, and other species of the versatile plant. In the

following weeks beans were also planted on the corn mounds. As the corn grew during the summer, the bean vines entwined themselves around thick stalks of corn.

Finally pumpkins, squashes, and watermelons were sown in separate patches. These fields separated the different varieties of corn, so the corn plants would not interbreed and lose their distinguishing characteristics. Weltfish explains: "There would be a planting of blue corn, then a pumpkin

The Natural World in Pawnee Lands

The valleys and grasslands of the Nebraska plains did not offer an abundance of natural resources to the Pawnee who lived there. In *The Roots of Dependency,* Richard White explains the environment of the Pawnee lands:

"The . . . Pawnee . . . lived in . . . three very different ecosystems: the tall-grass prairies, the river valleys, and the mixed-grass plains. . . .

[They] built their villages, planted their crops, and spent roughly half the year in . . . river valleys. The ecology of the Platte, Loup, and Republican [river] valleys where they lived was significantly different from [other rivers in the area]. Because these rivers were sandy streams with shifting beds, cottonwood . . . and willow . . . along with a few elm . . . dominated their banks. Over large areas, trees did not grow along the rivers but were confined to

the numerous islands of the Platte. Only in some of the smaller, less sandy feeder streams or in sheltered ravines could other species—principally green ash . . . American elm . . . black walnut . . . box-elder . . . and hackberry . . . survive and dominate.

In the absence of forest, several other plant communities dominated the bottomlands of the Platte and Loup. . . . [Numerous] swamps and marshes supported bulrushes . . . cattails . . . and other reeds . . . On slightly drier lands, tall coarse grasses such as prairie cordgrass . . . switchgrass . . . and Canada wild-rye . . . became numerous before yielding to Indian grass . . . and, much more commonly, to big bluestem. . . . Wild fruit trees and shrubs grew along ravines and streams or where bluffs afforded shelter. Sumac . . . hazel . . . wolfberry . . . buckbrush . . . wild plum . . . and prairie roses . . . were especially common."

Vegetable Varieties

Pawnee women skillfully cultivated a wide variety of corn, beans, and squash. They had at least fifteen varieties of corn, seven types of squash or pumpkins, and eight kinds of beans.

The Pawnee raised two major types of corn: flint, a hard-kernel corn used for cooking, and flour corn, which was ground for use in baking. They also raised sweet corn, which was cooked in its husk in a fire and eaten from the cob. Of these major species, there were several subspecies, including six types of flour corn in various colors such as black, white, yellow, red, blue, and speckled. There was also a variety of corn called Wonderful Corn that was not eaten but grown only for use in religious ceremonies.

The Pawnee also grew a wide variety of beans, whose names are listed in *The Lost Universe* by Gene Weltfish. Pawnee women grew "bean-red," "bean-white," "bean-yellow," "bean-head-black," "bean-head-red," "bean-spotted," and "bean-flat."

Squash and pumpkins also grew in various sizes and shapes. These were named after their colors or textures, such as "pumpkin-black" or "pumpkin-dry." One rounded squash was named "soft-buttock" for its resemblance to the human body.

The Pawnee raised three major types of corn—flint corn, sweet corn, and flour corn.

patch, then spotted corn, then a melon patch, and so on in this order."[12]

Tiring and Dangerous Toil

Pawnee women separated their fields with tall natural fences of sunflowers, which grew annually without being replanted. Sometimes women would argue over a piece of land and one might fence off her field with wooden stakes and buffalo-hide ropes. If one woman's planting failed to yield a decent crop, she might steal corn from her neighbors. This could lead to yelling, cursing, and even physical violence. More often than not, according to Weltfish, a poor woman could simply say to her neighbor, "I want you to take pity on me and give me some corn."[13]

In a typical Pawnee village, all mature women had at least one field between a half acre and one-and-a-half acres in size. Farming women were often helped in their labors by the young women of the household, who were either daughters or married to their sons.

Village chiefs assigned garden parcels to women, and land near villages was considered the most valuable. Richard White explains in *The Roots of Dependency:*

A woman was entitled to her field year after year for as long as she wished to use it, but it reverted to the village as a whole for reassignment at her death. This land was highly valued. The women planted only plots of disturbed soil [where humans or animals had tramped down the natural growth]—

most often found in the creek bottoms near the mouth of ravines—since such lands could be brought into production without the arduous work of breaking the sod. . . . To find such lands the women had to go seven or eight miles from the village, often locating their fields near natural springs.[14]

Working far from home was dangerous, as women could be attacked by an enemy tribe. In the 1860s, for instance, the Sioux were trying to take over Pawnee territory using fear and intimidation. Unarmed women farmers were prime targets: killing them created widespread grief and deprived families of food. In 1861, after Sioux warriors killed and scalped at least eighteen women of the Skidi subtribe, the Pawnee began to travel to their fields in large groups while young men patrolled the perimeters.

Collecting Wild Food

After the farmwork was done, women stopped by the river on their way home, rinsing off their hoes and jumping in the water for a bath. After the women were clean and refreshed, they gathered sticks of wood that had washed up on the riverbank to carry home for use as firewood.

After bathing, Pawnee women also searched for food. Many delicacies grew along the banks of the rivers, including wild onions, wild cucumbers, an herb called lamb's-quarters, and the prairie turnip, or Indian potato. Wild plums, persimmons, and chokecherries, which could be dried and preserved, also grew along riverbanks. The

The Platte River was a valuable resource for the Pawnee who fished its waters and gathered vegetables, herbs, fruits, and wetland grasses from its shores.

sweet thistle plant was peeled and eaten, and milkweed buds, prickly pear cactus, and rose hips were added to stews. Wetland grasses such as bulrush and cattails were collected and dried, their fibers used for weaving mats. Stiff porcupine grass was utilized for making brushes.

In addition to collecting wild fruits and vegetables on the riverbanks, the Pawnee fished the rivers for trout, crappie, and perch. The natives speared the fish or caught them in nets made from willow and rawhide. There were also several species of clams in the rivers that were used as meat while their shells were used as scrapers.

Preparing for the Buffalo Hunt

By June the corn was about three feet tall, and the village began to prepare for the summer buffalo hunt, a period of great uncertainty. For a typical Skidi hunt, over three thousand people from as many as six villages would travel as far as two hundred to three hundred miles for a period of four months. Along the way they might be attacked by enemies or not find large enough buffalo herds to sustain their population. It was a serious time of contemplation and also a period of hard work.

Pawnee men took particular care to gather proper weapons for the hunt. Guns were extremely expensive, and there were no sources of ammunition on the buffalo trail. For this reason hunters relied on the bow and arrow, which could be constructed or repaired on the move.

Bows were carved from the hard wood of the ash tree, and bowstrings were made from tightly rolled buffalo tendons known as sinew. Each hunter made his own bow and bowstring. The construction of straight-flying arrows from dogwood sticks, however, required the talents of

Pawnee hunters relied most on bows and arrows for hunting because rifles and ammunition were expensive.

Horses Bring Dramatic Change

Until the eighteenth century, the Pawnee did not have horses to help them hunt or move their belongings across the plains. In *The Buffalo Hunters*, Maggie Debelius and Stephanie Lewis describe how the introduction of horses around 1700 dramatically changed the Pawnee way of life.

"The horse transformed Plains nomadism from a life of [basic] subsistence into one of

The introduction of horses dramatically changed the Pawnee way of life.

abundance. Hunters could now pursue the buffalo much farther and faster than was ever possible on foot. They were capable of following the herds for scores of miles at almost any time of year, and the best of their horses could outrun even a stampeding buffalo. In a single day, it was possible for two or three mounted hunters to kill enough buffalo to provide 10 pounds of fresh meat daily for each member of a band of 100 persons for a week.

The horse was also a far more efficient beast of burden than the dog. It could pull a travois [a frame slung between trailing poles] laden with 300 pounds about 40 miles a day, or twice as far as the maximum distance a dog could haul a load one-fourth as heavy. The Indians could now carry larger reserves of food, amass more possessions, and sew larger [tepees]. Some tribes referred to the horse's abilities as a pack animal with wonder, calling it 'mystery dog,' 'medicine dog,' or 'sacred dog.'. . . As an additional bonus, the horse was herbivorous and grazed on the abundant prairie grass."

skilled craftsmen—and these men were in short supply. In 1867, for instance, only five arrow makers worked among the entire Skidi band of more than three thousand.

Every Pawnee hunter needed to place his order for arrows with one of the craftsman and

agree on trade goods for payment. Hunters also had to supply the arrow makers with straight, well-cured dogwood sticks. Weltfish writes of the rush to produce arrows before the hunt:

Practically the entire supply of arrows that [hunters] needed for the summer had to be made while they were still in the village as there was no time for such work while they were on the march or attacking the herd. A craftsman could produce about ten a day and he usually made them in lots of twenty, working them all in successive stages for the whole lot. . . . The hunter would consider twenty to forty arrows as a reasonable number to keep in his arsenal. In 1840 the Skidi population was estimated to have . . . 200 . . . adult hunters. . . . [This] would mean that each of the five craftsmen would have 40 of them to take care of, and supplying each with 20 arrows would mean that he had to produce 800 arrows to keep this group supplied. . . . This was 80 full days of work.[15]

The points of the arrow were the responsibility of individual hunters. Arrowheads were made from chipped flint and were often obtained by trade with other tribes. In the mid-1800s, however, the Pawnee began making arrowheads from iron barrel hoops that were brought to the area by white traders. The hoops were cut up by blacksmiths, and the hunters would sharpen them with metal files that were also brought in by traders. In the weeks before the hunt, almost every Pawnee man could be seen working on his supply of arrows.

Several days before the hunt was to commence, one of the village chiefs would climb to the top of his earth lodge and announce a departure day. At this time the hunters began their final preparations for leaving the village. They gathered together large sacks of tobacco and herbs so they would not run out of these sacred substances during the summer. In addition they had to make sure that their horses were prepared. Deerskin saddles had to be in good working condition, and large rawhide sacks for food and luggage were made ready to tie onto horses.

Meanwhile women packed enough food to sustain their families for the three weeks it would take to get to the hunting grounds. They packed dried vegetables, dried buffalo meat, corn, and beans. By the mid–nineteenth century a woman's food reserve might also include items from a trade store such as flour, coffee, sugar, and dried fruit.

Moving to the Hunting Grounds

When the Pawnee left their earth-lodge villages, the dusty trails quickly filled with thousands of people along with horses pulling travois—frames slung between trailing poles. Hundreds of dogs scamped underfoot. In 1870 George Bird Grinnell, a white author who traveled extensively with the Pawnee, described this procession in *Pawnee, Blackfoot and Cheyenne:*

At the time of which I am writing, the Pawnee had no wagons, all their possessions being transported on pack horses. . . . In packing the animals a bundle of lodge-poles is tied on either side of the saddle, one end projecting forward toward the horse's head, the other dragging on the ground behind. This is the *travois*. Cross poles are often tied between these two dragging bundles, and on these are carried packages of meat and robes. Often, too, on a robe stretched between them, a sick or wounded Indian, unable to ride, is transported. The lodge-poles having been fastened to the saddle, the lodge is folded up and placed on it between them, and blankets, robes, and other articles are piled on top of this, until the horse has on its back what appears to be about as much as it can carry. The pack is then lashed firmly in position, and pots, buckets and other utensils are tied about it wherever there is room.

The Pawnee transported their belongings using travois lashed to their saddles and dragged behind their horses.

On top of the load so arranged one or two women, or three or four children, clamber and settle themselves comfortably there, and the old horse is turned loose. . . . If the riders are women, each one holds a child or two in her arms. . . . If the living load consists of children, they have in their arms a lot of puppies; for puppies occupy with relation to the small Indian girls the place which dolls hold among the white children. Many of the pack animals are mares with young colts, and these last, instead of following quietly at their mothers' heels, range here and there. . . . Loose horses of all ages roam about at will, and their continual cries mingle with the barking of dogs, the calls of women, and the yells of boys, and make an unceasing noise.[16]

This noisy train of people and animals slowly moved to the buffalo hunting grounds found along the Republican River, on the border of present-day Nebraska and Kansas. During this journey of up to two hundred miles, the Pawnee set up a series of overnight encampments approximately ten miles apart.

Each night the women set up their tepees and—after this laborious task was completed—went out to gather firewood and water. Meanwhile, the men set out to hunt rabbit, quail, deer, elk, and antelope. After dinner was cooked and dishes were cleaned, hundreds of men, women, and children jumped into the river for a bath. In the morning the temporary villages were pulled down and the journey undertaken once again.

The traditional place for the final encampment was the confluence of Turkey Creek and the Republican River in southwestern Nebraska. As the Pawnee settled into this temporary village, the hunt could not begin until the elite men in the tribe killed ten or twenty buffalo to feed the thousands of people gathered. Weltfish explains: "This group of hunters included all the chiefs, other administrative officials and prominent men. The meat they obtained was widely distributed in the form of gifts and symbolized the fact that 'the chiefs feed the people buffalo meat.'"[17] After a feast, all hunters in the tribe would set out to hunt the huge buffalo herd.

The Kill

The buffalo hunt was a difficult and dangerous affair that had to be executed with great skill and patience. After scouts located the herds, they reported the location and numbers to the village elders, who assigned parties different areas in which to hunt.

Hunters used their understanding of buffalo behavior to help them with their task. In the summer, buffalo did not pack tightly together in herds. Instead they spread out over the grasslands and ate all morning. By noon many sat down and went to sleep in the midday sun. This was the best time to attack, and at a given signal the Pawnee hunters moved their horses into action. Each man picked out one or two buffalo to chase as the startled herd began to scatter.

Hunters picked their prey using various criteria. The skin of young buffalo calves was a perfect size for making children's robes. Buffalo around four years old were

Traveling Across Nebraska

The Pawnee made their journey across the harsh terrain of southern Nebraska without compasses or maps. In *The Lost Universe,* Gene Weltfish describes the trek to the hunting grounds:

"The westward journeys along the river banks [of the Loup] were relatively easy, but in turning southward the overland travel took them over deeply scarred irregular surfaces that were slow and hard to cross. North and south of the Loup the land surface consists of glacial [silt] blown into tall sandhills that look like dunes. To conduct a march across this terrain, especially loaded with baggage, is extremely difficult. Moreover, there are no identifiable landmarks, and it is easy to get lost. Both [the Platte and Loup] rivers have changed their courses numbers of times in the past and the marks of their winding fossil beds are deeply carved into the sandy layer, forming a series of shallow but sharply defined canyons and troughs.

The Pawnees had a detailed knowledge of every aspect of the land they would traverse. Its topography was in their minds like a series of vivid pictorial images, each a configuration where this or that event had happened in the past to make it memorable. This was especially true of the old men who had the richest store of knowledge in this respect. Their journey out was about ten miles a day and eight on the way back when they were more heavily laden with the dried meat. Anticipating these distances, they had to plan on stopping places where there was enough level land, wood for fuel, and available water for their whole large encampment of several thousand people and many more animals. They estimated the journey out as twenty days and the return journey twenty-seven days."

valued for their thick silken coats used for winter robes. Big buffalo were easiest to hunt because they were the slowest—and they also tasted best. The animal's hump was packed with fat and was considered a delicacy. Old buffalo were left alone—their meat was tough and stringy.

After choosing their buffalo, skilled hunters attempted to drive their quarry toward their camp, where the animal would be easier to butcher. Sometimes a running buffalo would charge right through the camp as women and children jumped out of the way and the older men tried to steer it back into the grasslands.

The Pawnee brought down the buffalo with arrows that were shot in rapid succession. Immediately after an animal was killed, the arduous task of processing the meat and hides began. The hide was cut along the backbone and along the belly and removed in two sections. The meat was cut first from one side and then the other along the backbone, ribs, and upper legs. The internal organs were then removed along with the tongue and brains. The heart and liver were often eaten raw by the hunter at this time.

The ribs were considered a delicacy and only eaten by men during ceremonies. Using the animal's foot and hoof as a hammer, the ribs were cracked off the backbone. If the animal was close to camp, other bones would be separated for later use in soup. If the kill was far from camp, the larger bones were regretfully left behind. The hide was then se-

cured to the back of the hunter's horse, and the meat and bones were artfully balanced and tied up for the journey back to camp.

The tired hunters returned to the camp around four o'clock in the afternoon, where they were met by excited villagers. As the men rested, the women began work on the hides and meat. The oldest women took several choice cuts of meat and began roasting them for quick snacks. Large slabs of meat were cut into steaks and dried on racks over fires. The dried meat was packed between layers of fat and tied up in sheets of rawhide.

Pawnee hunters carefully planned their buffalo hunts, waiting until the animals settled down after a morning of grazing.

In this manner, several thousand pounds of buffalo meat could be reduced to about eighty pounds.

No part of the animal was allowed to go to waste. Stirling lists the many uses the Pawnee found for buffalo.

The thick woolly hair of the buffalo was used to stuff leather-covered balls for ball games and to pad saddles; for weaving bags and ornaments; for making rope; for cushioning beds and back rests. . . .

The skin went into tepee covers, clothing, bags and other containers, cooking vessels, shields, saddles, and robes.

From the ribs were made skin scrapers, arrow points, gaming dice . . . and, when perforated, arrow straighteners. The shoulder blades were utilized for fleshing tools and axes, and . . . [hoes]. They were even used as an artist's palette for mixing paint. The leg bones became knives, awls . . . and hammers. . . .

Sinew was used for backing bows to increase their resilience, for sewing and for making strings. From the scrotum were made rattles and stirrup covers; from the bladder, water bags. The intestines were used for string and for bow rapping, the paunch for boiling water.

All the flesh, the organs, and the marrow in the bones were food. The fat served as a base for mixing paint. . . . Along with the brain and the liver, fat was used for tanning. Hoofs were turned into rattles

. . . and glue; gallstones into yellow paint. Blood and intestinal juices were used for a drink. The dried dung, famous "buffalo chips" of the prairie, was an important fuel.[18]

The Corn Harvest

While the Pawnee spent several months on the buffalo trail, the corn near the villages grew to a height of almost ten feet. By late August, the first ears were ready for roasting and drying. A few members of the tribe who could not travel, called the "leave behinds," tended to the summer fields. As September grew near, scouts rode in from the hunting ground to pick several dozen sample ears of corn. These would be brought back to the women in the hunting camps so they could be inspected for ripeness. When the hunt was over, the long trek home took about four weeks, as the horses were loaded down with tons of buffalo.

Instead of returning directly to their villages, the Pawnee set up their tepees close to their farm fields—the earth lodges were infested with fleas and mice after standing empty all summer. The ripe corn was at its peak and would have to be harvested before the women could fumigate their homes. As the harvest began, however, frequent trips were made back to the lodges for supplies.

The harvest began when senior women prepared corn-roasting pits inside their tepees. Meanwhile villagers went out to the fields to cut down the tall stalks of corn. The corn was shucked by the men, as the women roasted it over hot coals. When it cooled, the husks were removed and the kernels were scraped off the cob with a clamshell. This laborious task continued for three weeks, during which time an average village harvested 400 acres of corn yielding 10,000 bushels, or approximately 40,000 dry gallons of produce.

As the final ears of corn were harvested, workers shifted their attention to the beans, walking through the fields all day bent at the waist to pick beans off the vines. For processing, the beans were dried in the hot sun after being spread out on tanned hides. After the beans were harvested, the pumpkins were brought in from the fields. The pulp was scraped from the skin and eaten. The skin was cut into circular strips that were dried on racks over fire pits. These strips were later used as material to weave mats.

As with the buffalo, nothing was wasted and every bit of the harvest was used in some manner. An elder named Old-Man-That-Chief commented: "In the old days . . . grandma would see an ear of corn or a single bean lying on the ground and she would be half-crying to see it lying there [going to waste]."[19]

Fall and Winter

As the days grew short and the night winds turned sharp, the work of the harvest drew to a close. The summer's bounty of dried

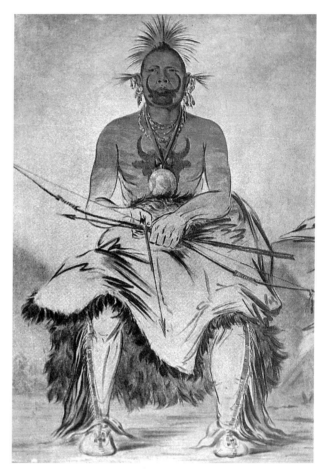

A Pawnee hunter, face and chest decorated with images of a buffalo, is ready for the hunt.

buffalo meat, corn, beans, and pumpkins was piled high in storage tepees. Women cleaned and fumigated the earth lodges while the men hauled the great stores of food back to the villages. As the food was laid into pits beneath the lodges, the Pawnee began planning their autumn rituals, which would last thirty days.

The short blustery days ahead would be filled with a plentiful supply of food, and the long cold nights filled with storytelling and jokes. Women would spend time making clothing and carving bowls.

By early November it was time to once again leave village life behind and set out on the winter buffalo hunt. This was the most grueling work of all, trudging across the prairie while the winds howled. Horses could barely get enough to eat as a white blanket of snow covered the grasslands. By the time the hunt was over in February, many horses died from starvation. For the Pawnee, however, the frigid winter hunt was just another part of the circle of the seasons. As winter drew to a close, they would return heavily laden with buffalo meat to the warming fires of their earth lodges. Soon the spring rains would come and melt the snow, and another year would begin for the Pawnee people on the Nebraska plains.

Chapter 3

Spirits, Priests, and Ceremonies

The end of the Pawnee year came when the people returned to their villages in February after the winter buffalo hunt. As the winter snow melted and the first signs of spring came to the plains, the new year began. With the new year came a series of religious ceremonies, rites, and rituals that lasted until the summer buffalo hunt was to begin. After the hunt, during the autumn harvest season, a new round of ceremonies marked the days until the coming of winter.

The Pawnee believed that their natural surroundings were filled with spirits that lived in all plants, animals, rocks, and weather phenomena. These spirits were ruled by the supreme deity, Tirawa, which in the Pawnee's Caddoan language means "pervasive ocean-of-power investing the universe." Grinnell explains how the animals interacted with Tirawa—and the Pawnee:

The fishes which swim in the rivers, the birds of the air and the beasts which roam over the prairie, have sometimes intelligence, knowledge and power far beyond those of man. But they are not gods. Their miraculous attributes are given them by [Tirawa], whose servants they are, and who often makes them the medium of his communications to man. They are his messengers—his angels—and their powers are always used for good. . . . Prayers are made to them; sometimes for direct help in time of need, but more often for intercession.[20]

This powerful world of gods and spirits touched every aspect of Pawnee life and gave the people a rich source of strength and purpose. And the Pawnee believed that Tirawa had given them control over the natural world. As White writes: "The Pawnees believed that they annually recreated and renewed the earth and maintained its existence through their ceremonies."[21]

Cardinal and Semicardinal Directions

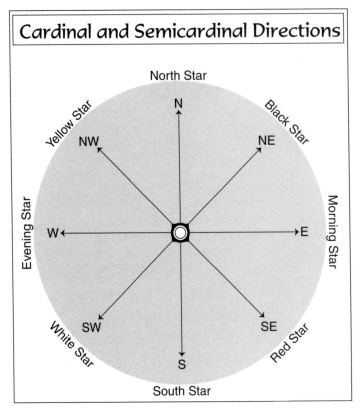

The stars and four cardinal directions created by Tirawa, the Pawnee supreme deity.

sun as a helper. The North Star and the South Star filled the other two directions, while other important stars were the Black Star (northeast), Yellow Star (northwest), Red Star (southeast), and White Star (southwest).

These stars held up the heavens, and Evening Star created the earth using lightning, wind, and rain— tools given to her by Tirawa. After Evening Star had created the waters, timbers, and seeds, Morning Star convinced her to mate with him, and together they created the first human being, a girl. Later the Moon and Sun mated to create the first boy. Both children were born on a cloud and carried to earth by tornadoes. When these two matured, they had a boy and girl. Evening Star instructed these children in their respective roles in life. According to Weltfish:

[The] girl is the fruitfulness of the earth, the form of the earth lodge, the nature of speech and of the land outside. The man got the clothing of a warrior and shown the way to travel over the earth, how to make war and how to hunt; he was also taught his role in the act of procreation.[23]

Evening Star Creates the World

According to Pawnee belief, Tirawa lived in heaven and created the universe and the stars, from which all other life originated. It is said that Tirawa placed the most important stars in the four cardinal directions. In the west was the Evening Star, known today as Venus, who according to Weltfish was "a beautiful woman, Goddess of the Night and Germination,"[22] who was given the moon as a companion. In the east lived the Morning Star—or Mars—who had the

After a time the population of the earth increased, and Evening Star periodically came down to earth to teach her grandchildren the story of creation and sacred songs.

Sacred Bundles

As the population grew, the original people ventured out farther and farther to hunt, and soon discovered there were other villages in the world. The first boy born to the Sun and Moon, named First Man, invited the people of these other villages to a great council meeting at a place called Center Village. During this time, First Man became known as Chief of Center Village. When the visitors from other villages arrived, Chief of Center Village created gifts for the guests called sacred bundles, which were made from powerful magical and spiritual objects. The people were instructed by Evening Star and Morning Star to follow a yearly cycle of ceremonies and songs using these sacred bundles, which derived their powers from the stars and became central to worship among the Pawnee.

As a result of the legends, every village had its own special bundle, and sacred medicine bundles were found in every earth lodge. Important individuals such as warriors, chiefs, and dancers had their own bundles. The bundles were kept for years and were often blackened by wood smoke and age. Items within were believed to contain concentrated sacred power. White describes one such bundle, viewed by an unnamed white man in 1830:

[It contained] a buffalo robe, fancifully dressed, skins of several fur bearing animals . . . the skull of a wild cat, stuffed skins of a sparrowhawk . . . and the swallow-tailed fly catcher, several bundles of scalps and broken arrows taken from enemies, a small bundle of Pawnee arrows, some ears of corn and a few wads of buffalo-hair, such as may be found in wallows where the animals roll when moulting.[24]

Pawnee religious ceremonies utilized sacred items contained within the bundles. Village bundles were opened during the first thunder of spring, a time signifying Evening Star's creation of earth from storms. Special priests were in charge of the holiest bundles, and these men were the most powerful in the tribe. Some bundles had specific items carrying special powers: the war bundle, for instance, might contain pieces of human skull from a vanquished enemy; the medicine bundle might contain herbs to heal the sick.

The Power of the Priests and Chiefs

The Pawnee believed that their chiefs and priests were able to express the desires of the gods on earth, and only these respected men could properly utilize the powers of the bundles. And while there was a distinction between the role of chief and that of priest, chiefs often acted as priests, but priests were not necessarily chiefs.

Whatever their title, the holy men were regarded as shining stars from the heavens who walked upon the earth and acted as fathers and protectors of the Pawnee people. White explains how priests obtained these powers:

Medicine men were called in to heal the sick but were also believed to use witchcraft.

These men passed their standing on to their sons so that the chiefs and priests formed an hereditary elite. Their rank as chiefs was a birthright; their actual power within the nation, however, depended on their knowledge and behavior.

Meaningful political power in the society came only to those of the proper rank who either displayed knowledge of the bundles or manifested the power embodied in them. . . . The necessary knowledge of the bundles was not easily acquired. To gain it, the aspiring priest had to serve a long apprenticeship to another priest, usually a kinsman, to whom he gave gifts in exchange for knowledge. The older

priest, however, always held back some of the secrets of the bundles and communicated them only when ready to die.[25]

While chiefs might use their powers for religious purposes, people also looked to them for their wisdom and regal bearing, which was believed to be an expression of heavenly power. Chiefs were expected to remain thoughtful and stoic under pressure. Preston Holder describes the qualities required of a Pawnee chief in *The Hoe and the Horse on the Plains:*

They were men to whom violence was a stranger; they were quiet and secure in the knowledge of their power. Their voices were never raised in anger or threatened violence. The image was one of large knowledge, infinite quiet patience, and thorough understanding. There was no outward show of authority; such was not needed. . . . These were secure, calm, well-bred, gracious men whose largess was noted and who had no need to shout of their strength.[26]

Such men were deeply respected among the people, and their decisions were final even if there was opposition among the tribe.

The Cycle of Ceremonies

The knowledge held by the priests and chiefs was crucial to the cycle of cere-

monies that were central to Pawnee life, for few acts of basic survival were conducted without some sort of religious ritual. According to White:

> It was the ceremonies that ensured that the corn grew and the buffalo could be hunted. For the Pawnees' world to prosper, the power of the sky had to vitalize the earth to produce life and plenty. All the rituals surrounding agriculture and the hunt reflected an attempt to procure this life-giving contact.[27]

Each ceremony featured its own sacred bundles, songs, dances, and prayers. Many

Doctors and Healing

Pawnee doctors, sometimes known as medicine men or shamans, took their powers not from the stars but from animals, herbs, and other earthly manifestations of the spirits. While shamans were often called in to heal the sick, the Pawnee believe that healers could also cause death and misery using black magic or evil sorcery, thrusting a "witch pellet" into a person by sleight of hand. In *The Lost Universe*, Gene Weltfish explains how a shaman healed one chief by making him throw up the "witch pellet":

"When the doctor was called in he would say, 'You seem to have some kind of cold, but something else may be in your stomach.' The

doctor makes medicine in a big bucket of water. He tells the patient to drink and see if it can come up. . . . The patient has to drink a whole lot before he can throw up. Then when he says he has enough, they tickle his throat with a feather, telling him to stand up. Maybe it doesn't come up yet and the doctor tells him, 'Take all the medicine.' Then at last the person doubles up and the fragments of the witch-pellet come up. The doctor says, 'Look, here, this is it. A bad person gave you this. . . .' The doctor says, 'Throw it (the poison pellet) into the fire,' but the witch [who is still there] suggests they throw it outside where he can retrieve it. Someone who knows better finally induces them to burn it up."

his daily food and also the object of his most profound reverence and worship."[28]

Every warrior who left the village to fight a battle wore a sacred ear of corn on his left shoulder. When Pawnee men visited other tribes on peace or trading missions, they carried ears of sacred corn as symbols of the universe. And the most important corn was the two ears found in every sacred bundle. The ears each had individual names, and they were thanked by women before every meal for the food they were about to eat.

The first corn ceremony of the year was the Spring Renewal, held in March. This ritual was performed at the time of the first thunder from the south and was the most important ceremony, attended by the mother of all Pawnee, in the form of the Evening Star sacred bundle.

The Sacred Corn ritual was held in late April when a special type of corn seed was given to all the owners of sacred bundles. This corn was planted but never eaten. When mature, its ears would be placed in the bundles. The second corn ceremony of the year was the Ground-breaking Ceremony. Until this ritual was completed in early May, no corn could be planted. The highlight of this ceremony was an energetic pantomime of breaking the ground with sacred buffalo hoes that were kept in special bundles for this purpose. The morning after the Ground-breaking Ceremony, the first food corn was planted. The final spring ceremony, Young Mother Corn, was held to encourage the budding corn to grow strong and healthy through-

The rank of chief was hereditary among the Pawnee.

ceremonies were held to give thanks for the sacred corn that was used for both physical and spiritual sustenance. As Weltfish writes: "To the Pawnee, the ear of corn was

out the summer while the tribe was away on the buffalo hunt.

Sacred Autumn Rituals

After the summer buffalo hunt, corn ceremonies resumed during the autumn harvest. Fall corn ceremonies mirrored their spring counterparts—for each ritual performed during planting, a ceremony with a similar theme was held at harvest.

The first fall celebration was the Green Corn Ceremony. Like the Spring Renewal, it was overseen by the Evening Star bundle. The ceremony was performed when the Pawnee were about to move back into their earth lodges after the summer buffalo hunt.

The Sacred Seed Ceremony

In *Pawnee Hero Stories and Folk Tales*, a nineteenth-century elder named Curly Chief explains the dance of the Sacred Seed Ceremony to author George Bird Grinnell:

"The preparations for this dance are always made by a woman. . . . In making ready for the dance, she must furnish the dried meat made from the whole of a buffalo, fat and lean, every part of it. The sack which holds the heart she dries, and fills it with all the kinds of corn—the five colors, the blue corn, which represents the blue sky, the red corn, which stands for the evening sunset, the yellow corn, which typifies the morning sunrise, the white corn, which stands for a white cloud, and the spotted corn, which represents the sky dotted with clouds. . . .

When the day has come . . . the high priest stands at the back of the lodge with the sacred bundles . . . before him. Then this leading woman comes forward, and presents to the high priest the dried meat and the sack

of corn, and two ancient, sacred hoes, made from the shoulder-blade of a buffalo. . . . She places them on the ground before the sacred bundles, the corn in the middle, and the two hoes on either side. With these things she also presents a sacred pipe, filled and ready for lighting, taken from a sacred bundle. . . .

The old high priest . . . prays . . . and lights the sacred pipe, blowing smoke to heaven, to the earth, and to the four points of the compass. . . . Then the leading woman steps forward. . . . She takes the bag of corn, and . . . stands in a particular position . . . holding the bag of corn up to the sky in both her hands. . . .

After these ceremonies the women come forward, holding their hoes in their hands, and dance about the lodge one after another in single file. . . . These ceremonies and the songs and prayers were to ask for a blessing on the hunt and on the corn, and to learn whether they would be blessed in both."

The Evening Star priest oversaw this ritual as respected warriors and tribal elders feasted on green corn. The Evening Star bundle was opened, and the sacred pipe within was smoked by the men, with the pipe stem pointed at the celestial gods in the sky. The contents of the bundle were passed over an incense made of sweet grass, and an offering of corn was made to the heavens. This process continued with all the other sacred bundles in a village.

The second ceremony of autumn, the Mature Mother Corn ritual, was celebrated while the mature corn was being gathered from the fields. To perform the ceremony, women removed all beds and furniture from an earth lodge. Before dawn the lodge's bundle was taken to the sacred corn fields, where ears of holy corn were placed within it. As Weltfish writes, "These would replace the old Mother Corn ears in the sacred bundles. In this way the sacred bundles always contained some fertile seeds."[29] Later the people assembled in the lodge of a priest, and each woman brought her finest ears of sacred corn to be piled on the north side of the structure and separated by color. Beans and squash were also donated.

The women left the lodge and the men sang four songs for each of the cardinal directions—north, south, east, and west. A final song was sung to the new Mother Corn. The priest hugged an ear of corn to his breast, then passed it to the next man. He hugged it and passed it around the lodge in a circle, until all the men had embraced the new Mother Corn.

Another song was sung that symbolically raised the voice of the corn to the heavens. The corn was passed around one more time, and each man at the ceremony blew his breath on it four times to symbolize new life. The old corn that had been replaced in the sacred bundle was kept by warriors to guarantee success in battle, or held by traders who believed that it would ensure successful transactions.

The Four Pole Ceremony, the final ritual of fall, was meant to commemorate the harvest and unite all Pawnee people under Tirawa. The ceremony was conducted within a large round building constructed specially for this purpose. Inside the sacred structure, four posts were erected, each symbolizing a semicardinal direction—that is, southwest, southeast, northwest, and northeast. These posts represented the entire earth and all people upon it.

Each pole was a different color and came from a different type of wood. The White Pole was from cottonwood and was set in the southwest. The Yellow Pole was made from willow and was planted in the northwest. The Red Pole was set in the southeast and made from box elder. The Black Pole was cut from elm and set in the northeast. The ceremony was conducted in two parts: first a war party set out in four different directions to obtain the poles. When they returned, according to Weltfish, the chief recalled "certain events in the creation ritual that represented the essential nature of the world."[30]

The Morning Star Ritual

While many tribes held elaborate ceremonies concerning corn, the Pawnee had one unique ritual involving human sacrifice that they inherited from their ancestors in Mexico.

Before the Pawnee tribes migrated to Nebraska from east Texas, they are believed to have been part of the Aztec tribes who once ruled Mexico. Some of their religious tenets—such as the belief that the stars were gods—appear to be Mexican in origin. And while human sacrifice is highly unusual among North American Indian tribes, it was an integral part of Aztec religious ceremonies. The Skidi band of the Pawnee also performed such an act at the Morning Star Ceremony.

The Skidi believed that in return for fathering the human race, Morning Star demanded the sacrifice of a thirteen-year-old girl. As the first star of day, Morning Star was the supreme male deity, bringing light to the world when he mated with Evening Star, who lived in darkness. The Skidi believed that the Morning Star Ceremony guaranteed the renewal of all life on earth and prevented the sun from burning up the planet. This made the Morning Star ritual a profoundly important ceremony. This ritual was not performed annually, however, but only every three to five years. The Skidi relied on special dreams and cosmic visions as signals to perform the Morning Star Ceremony, as described in *The Buffalo Hunters* by Maggie Debelius and Stephanie Lewis:

The prerequisite to the ceremony was the conjunction of two events: A member of the Skidi band of the Pawnee had to dream of the morning star—or a personification of it—and

subsequently arise from sleep to actually see the planet coming up over the eastern horizon. The dreamer would then go, in tears, to consult with the priest of the morning star bundle. As soon as he saw the man crying, the priest would put his arm around him, and he, too, would break down. The two men cried because they were obligated to do what the morning star commanded even though both of them knew that it was wrong: They had to sacrifice a human being.[31]

At this time, a special warrior's costume and other sacred objects were removed from the Morning Star bundle. The clothes were later donned by a leader, who gathered other braves and led them on an expedition to an enemy camp to kidnap an adolescent girl.

When an enemy camp was located, a special ceremony commenced that centered on songs, the sacred bundle, and the smoke from the campfire, which was viewed as an offering to Morning Star. The Pawnee surrounded the enemy camp, and the leader approached from the east while the rest of the tribe invaded from the southeast. When the Morning Star rose above the horizon, the leader signaled the attack by imitating the cry of the wolf. Colin F. Taylor describes the kidnapping of the girl:

[Warriors were] reminded not to kill unless necessary but to find a suitable young captive and pronounce her . . . "holy" for the Morning Star. Generally, little attempt was made at pursuit by the enemy tribe as there was a feeling that this was a kind of cosmic destiny, although retribution could (and often did) come later in the form of a war party against the entire Pawnee tribe.[32]

Death of a Maiden

The captive was taken back to the Skidi village and given over to the priest, who represented the wolf, an animal believed to be responsible for spreading death throughout the world. The young girl was pampered, fed, and kept ignorant of her fate for weeks, or even months, until the Skidi priests decided that the time was right for the sacrifice.

The Morning Star ritual was a four-day affair that included the mournful singing of twenty-one different songs. In the darkness just before dawn on the fourth day, the young maiden was led to a scaffold that had been specially constructed for the ritual. Stirling describes the culmination of the ceremony:

> The right half of the girl's body was painted red and the left half black, and a fan shaped eagle-feather headdress was attached to her hair. She was led to the scaffold, everything possible being done to conceal her fate from her.
>
> The procession was timed so that the arrival at the scaffold corresponded with the rising of the Morning Star. If the girl mounted the scaffold of her own will, it was considered an especially favorable omen.
>
> The girl was lashed to the scaffold, and as soon as the star appeared over the horizon, a small group of warriors sprang from concealment and rushed towards the scaffold as if attacking an enemy.
>
> The man who made the capture shot an arrow from close range through the heart of the victim, using a bow and sacred arrow from the medicine bundle. Every male in the tribe then shot an arrow into her body, fathers or male relatives pulling bows for boys too small to do so themselves.[33]

After the ritual was concluded, the body was carried out onto the prairie and laid down facing the Morning Star. The entire village then spent the next three days feasting, dancing, and singing.

Historians say that the Pawnee never liked performing the Morning Star Ceremony but felt an obligation to their principal deity to continue with the practice. It was finally halted around 1840 when a highly respected Pawnee warrior cut the young maiden free at the last moment before death. He pulled her onto his horse and took her back to her tribe. When he returned to his village, instead of facing punishment, he was lauded for his courage. Having broken the sacrificial cycle that had been in place for centuries, the Morning Star Ceremony came to an end. In later years, the ritual continued but without human sacrifice.

A Home in the Universe

The Pawnee had several more important yearly ceremonies by which they measured their days. In fact, there were few aspects of life that did not have accompanying rituals

Ceremonial Dancing

All Pawnee ceremonies were marked by hours of dancing. In *The Mystic Warriors of the Plains,* Thomas E. Mails explains ceremonial dancing:

"Many of the [Pawnee] dances were religious ceremonials, whose intent was to gain wisdom from or give thanks to the supernatural powers. . . . There were cosmic, healing, peace, victory, mourning, and hunting dances, dances of a purely social type, and . . . planting and harvest dances. Some dances were performed exclusively by men, and some solely by women. In other instances men and women danced together. Some dances were held in which anyone might take part, and others were limited to a single dancer selected for the occasion. Many dances . . . were private property, and could only be performed by their rightful owners. Each of the [tribes] had dances that centered on the themes of mystery and war. Some dances to be used while curing the sick were owned by individual holy men, and some by societies of medicine men. However, it should also be pointed out that every ritual was not a dance, and the word 'dance' has often been wrongly applied by White men to some of the great Indian rituals in which dancing actually played but a small part. . . .

All Indian dances followed traditional forms. Some of the dance steps were simple, but others were complicated and quite difficult to learn. And the male style differed from the female. When men danced the heel and ball of each foot in turn was lifted and brought down with considerable force, so as to produce a thudding sound. The changes of their position were slow, but the shifts in attitude were rapid and sometimes violent. Women employed the shuffle, the glide, the hop, and the leap. Usually, dancers moved in a clockwise circle direction, 'with the sun.' When dancing with the men, women were usually placed in an inside circle."

The Pawnee had a ritual dance for every occasion.

As a young warrior, Chief Petalesharo showed great courage which brought the ancient Morning Star Ceremony to an end.

Viewing the sky was so important that the Pawnee designed their earth lodges so they could view the Evening Star in the western sky through the central smoke hole. The Morning Star could be seen through the east-facing doorway. Weltfish explains:

The house was a microcosm of the universe and as one was at home inside, one was also at home in the outside world. For the dome of this sky was the high-arching roof of the universe and the horizon all around was the circular wall of the cosmic house. Through the roof of the house the star gods poured down their strength from their appropriate directions in a constant stream.[34]

or ceremonies. To the isolated Pawnee villagers out under the twinkling starry skies of the Nebraska grasslands, the universe was rich with spiritual meaning.

From the cosmic light show in the heavens to the stick-and-mud roofs of their earth lodges, the Pawnee gained the power and strength to fruitfully survive for centuries.

Chapter 4

Men, Women, and Families

The Pawnee believed that every member of the tribe was descended from the goddess Evening Star. Their belief in a common lineage meant that the Pawnee saw themselves as members of one big family with each person related to all the others. Young children referred to all older women as their "grandmothers." A man not only called his real mother *atira*, or "my mother," but also used that term for his mother's sisters, and also the sisters of his father and their daughters. In this way one person could extend his or her family ties to almost every earth lodge in a village.

Women at the Center of Life

Women held a special place in Pawnee society. They were considered the heads of their families as well as of their households, giving them great influence in tribal affairs.

When a man married, he moved into the lodge of his wife's mother. If the couple later decided to separate, the man moved back into his own mother's lodge. And within that lodge, the oldest woman held the most power. As White explains:

> The real center of the Pawnee family and lodge was the senior woman. The occupants of a lodge consisted of a woman, her husband, her unmarried children, her married daughters and their husbands, sometimes her married sons, her grandchildren, and more distant kin. Here the Pawnees organized the productive activities of the village; here the center of everyday life was fixed.[35]

As the center of activity within a village, the senior women oversaw the division of goods such as corn, meat, skins, trade goods, and other products. In this way the wealth of the village was distributed evenly within kinships, and no one was denied sustenance in spite of his or her advanced age, physical inability to contribute, or other problems.

Family Relationships

Just as almost all mature females were referred to as *atira* by a large group of people, the *atira* and other women referred to dozens of individuals as *piirau*, or "child," no matter what that person's age or relationship. And in a sense, every person had many women to "mother" them.

The birth mother was accorded profound respect, however. The relationship between birth mothers and their children was very formal. Pawnee children did not roughhouse, whine, or make childish demands in the presence of the birth mother. She, in turn, instructed her child in the lessons of life, religion, and death. If children wanted

Distribution of Goods

Among the Pawnee, senior women in each lodge controlled the family's wealth of food, skins, and trade goods. But as Richard White writes in *The Roots of Dependency*, much of a village's wealth eventually ended up in the hands of the chief:

"It was the mark of chiefs to give to their people. When able, they gave freely, and it was their particular duty to provide personally for the destitute. Accepting the gift of a chief did not normally involve an obligation to reciprocate.

Reciprocal giving between chiefs and people would have been redundant in Pawnee society since the whole structure of the village channeled goods upward. They flowed toward the [sacred] bundles and those who controlled the bundles. During the major ceremonial feasts of the year, the people gave gifts to the celebrants—the priests and chiefs—whose knowledge of the bundles brought prosperity to the people. The power that chiefs and priests derived from the medicine bundles greatly ramified the occasions for giving. Gifts came to the chiefs and priests as a payment for knowledge, as thanksgiving to the powers for success in war or the hunt, and as part of numerous other occasions in daily life. At feasts, the first invited were the chiefs and priests. . . .

From this constant upward flow of goods, the chiefs acquired the presents that they gave to the people. Most wealth paused only briefly at the top of the Pawnee hierarchy; a chief's unwillingness to give would have meant his loss of influence since his greed would have violated the very code that assured him of his power. As wealth filtered back down, however, the best goods—those which possessed highest quality or which gave symbolic status . . . remained with those of the highest social standing."

Pawnee women were considered the heads of their families and households and they wielded considerable influence in tribal affairs.

to play, solve small problems, or ask insignificant questions, they went to the grandmother, who treated them with the warmth and easygoing intimacy normally associated with mothers in modern times.

The relationship between fathers and their children was also formal. Pawnee were careful to always conduct themselves appropriately and show their fathers proper respect. When visiting, for instance, adult sons showed respect by bringing their fathers a supply of buffalo, deer, rabbit, or any other meat available.

Relationships between grandfathers and their grandchildren were less formal than between fathers and children. Boys joked and wrestled with their maternal grandfathers, and the older men in turn instructed youngsters in the tough lessons of life. A grandfather, for instance, might pluck his grandson from his warm bed on a cold winter morning and throw him into the frigid creek in order to mold him into a tough warrior. In turn, children and young adults had much more relaxed and intimate relationships with their grandfathers than with their fathers.

Fathers and Children

The Pawnee lived in a closed world where every person who was not an enemy was considered some sort of relative. And each kin designation came with a specific set of rules for social etiquette. In *The Lost Universe*, Gene Weltfish explains how these concepts worked in daily life:

"There were no normal interpersonal relations among the Pawnees that did not carry with them a kin designation. People with whom one dealt as equals had to be placed in some kin category; lack of such a relation could only imply slave or enemy status. In the various trade or gift exchange ceremonials that were conducted between tribes or bands, a whole kin structure was built up so that they could communicate on a peaceful level. The most notable example was the Calumet or Peace Pipe Ceremony, in which the visiting trade party represented Fathers, while the ones they visited were designated their Children. Many of the ceremonial acts were designed to carry out this idea. There was no way of communicating with peaceful strangers unless they were fitted into the kin structure, and it is for this reason that the President of the United States is referred to as the Great White Father and that white friends are adopted into the tribe."

Marriage Customs

All Pawnee, no matter what their age or status, were tied together by kinship and marriage. By modern standards, the Pawnee had unusual marriage customs—young girls around the age of fifteen often married men age forty and older. Because mature men had more hunting and combat experience than younger men, they were considered better marriage choices for young girls. As Weltfish writes: "A man contracted a marriage in terms of services he could render to the family of the girl that he married. Normally he was expected to come to live in her household and 'take care of them,' [that is], render them major services."[36]

When a man married a young woman and moved into her earth lodge, he was referred to by the Pawnee with a word that meant "the one who is sitting among us." The man referred to his in-laws as *tutukaku*, "I sit inside for you" or "I am in this house for your benefit." A man formally referred to his wife with the word that meant "I own her," but the more affectionate term was *tsustit*, or "old lady." The wife in turn called her husband *karahus*, or "old man."[37]

Some Pawnee marriages were monogamous, meaning one man married one woman. Polygamy, or the custom of having multiple marriage partners, was also permitted. Polygamous relationships arose when a man lived in the earth lodge of his wife and later decided to marry one or more of her younger sisters when the women came of age. Debelius and Lewis explain the situation:

Sisters-in-law made natural choices for additional wives because they were of the same family lineage as the first wife. Thus, no conflict arose as to where the family should live. Nor did Plains women consider it degrading to share their husbands with other wives. A first wife usually welcomed the appearance of the second wife in her home for the daily companionship of another woman and to reduce her workload.[38]

Women might also take more than one husband, sometimes marrying a man and then later marrying his younger brother or nephew.

Mature Pawnee men were considered good marriage choices for young girls because they had more hunting and combat experience than younger men.

Multiple Marriages

With young girls marrying older men, marriages between young men and older women were common. Weltfish explains:

Because of the services [to the household] required on both sides, a young man would have little alternative but to marry a capable older woman, and a young girl who was in no position to carry the responsibilities of a mature woman would normally marry a mature man. The situation finally reversed itself when, after a marriage to an older man, the woman attains maturity and the competence to maintain a household. She is now in a position to choose a handsome young man as a second husband. The young man on his part finally gains maturity at the age of forty and can [ask] for the hand of a young girl of fifteen and join a household where his capabilities will be appreciated.[39]

Young men often found mature women to marry at the earth lodge of an uncle. This is a result of a custom in which a young Pawnee boy often had a closer relationship with his mother's brother than with his own father.

It was quite common for a boy to move into his uncle's house around the age of ten, and according to Weltfish, "assumed the role of apprentice husband and eventually, when he came of age, of junior husband. He called his uncle's wives 'wife' and the children of his uncle . . . 'my child.'"[40] In such a case, the twenty-year-old grown child of the uncle called his ten-year-old cousin "father" and treated him with respect given to a real father.

When the young boy matured, he could propose marriage to one of his uncle's mature wives.

Pawnee marriage practices gave children the security of having several mothers and fathers under the same roof. In some cases, several brothers might live together sharing several wives—who might be sisters. In this situation the children called all the adults in their household "mother" or "father," and all children were considered the responsibility of all the adults. As one unnamed Pawnee said: "We think a child should not be too closely bound to its own mother, for should she have to be away or should she die, it would break the child's heart."[41]

Arranging for Marriage

To ensure (as much as possible) a successful marriage, the men of the tribe arranged most marriages. This process included an assessment of the ages and abilities of the two people proposed for a potential coupling. Fathers and brothers often engaged in intense negotiations. Since Pawnee only married people from their own villages, the family relationship between man and woman was thoroughly discussed. While women sometimes married their cousins or even grandfathers, such close marriages were frowned upon because a divorce might tear a family apart.

No matter what a man's age or relation, when he wanted to marry, he was expected to show his intentions by giving many gifts, especially horses, to his prospective in-laws. The father and brothers of a desirable bride might be given six horses, for example.

When a Pawnee woman accepted the arranged marriage, her future mother-in-law organized a group of female relatives to hold a group corn planting. Weltfish describes this ceremony:

As many as twenty-five women would be gathered in [the mother-in-law's] field and they would go to her house and get her seeds and line up in the field ready to plant. The field, about "half a block" long, was hoed and planted by the women more or less in unison while two old women sat at the far end singing a song from one of the sacred bundles ceremonies:

You are just hoeing around,
Big ground, lucky ground.

They were arranged in rows and while the women sang they made the mounds. Then they put in the seeds and then they all went to the home of the daughter-in-law[,] where they were entertained at a feast of corn and dried buffalo meat.[42]

Birth of a Child

With marriage came children, and the prospective birth of a Pawnee child was surrounded by many important rituals and cere-

The Pawnee carried their babies on cradleboards which were made by the father's sisters and presented to the mother as a symbol of respect and honor.

monies. When a woman became pregnant, she began to take long walks in the early morning, because it was believed that this helped the baby grow. Before the child was born, the mother or grandmother stitched together two beaded magical objects, one in the shape of a sand lizard, the other a turtle. Mails describes the look and importance of these amulets:

Every member of a Pawnee family was involved with the birth and raising of the children.

These were gracefully shaped, and finished with horsehair or [bird] feathers attached to the ends of the four legs. Both animals were revered because they "lived forever" and were so difficult to kill. Their protective power was enlisted early as a guardian and guarantee of the individual's long life. When the child was born, the umbilical cord was cut and placed inside the turtle, packed in tobacco or herbs, while the lizard served as a decoy to lure away malevolent forces. A second use of the turtle was to remind the bearer that his life was a precious gift from his parents, and he had the responsibility to marry and to pass the gift of birth and life on to his own children.

When the child began to walk, that amulet was attached to his clothing to serve as a constant reminder of its purpose. . . . Sometimes the turtle was put away later on and other times it was kept by the mother. A boy often tied it to the left shoulder of his shirt, and then transferred it to his buffalo-horned headdress if he became a renowned warrior.[43]

While the mother or grandmother sewed the amulets, the father's sisters made a cradle-board to carry the child after birth. This item was as important as the amulets because it demonstrated the respect and honor that the sisters-in-law held for the mother.

When a child was born, the woman simply gave birth in her earth lodge. If the tribe was out on a buffalo hunt, the baby was born alongside the trail. Older women acted as midwives and helped with the delivery, and priests were called in to sing ceremonial songs to ensure a healthy birth. If there was trouble, the priest added a special charm to the turtle amulet, to protect the baby and mother from harm.

Magical Names

After a child was born, he or she was given a name at a special ceremony. The Pawnee never referred to each other by their personal names, however, and used only kinship names, such as uncle or mother, under most circumstances. Names were considered titles of honor that were only bestowed for the most intimate of reasons and were not to be shared with anyone else. As Matthew W. Stirling explains in "Indians of Our Western Plains," in *National Geographic:*

"[Names] were believed to possess magical virtues. When a child was born, the parents usually selected an old person, preferably one with many achievements, to bestow a name. The [Pawnee] did not inherit the family names. . . . In the case of a boy, his first name was retained until adolescence, when frequently a new name would be bestowed upon him.

When, as an adult, he had an unusual dream or performed some noteworthy deed, his name would again be changed, not once, but sometimes several times. As a rule, girls retained their first names throughout life. Marriage did not alter a woman's name. . . . Individuals in most tribes were never addressed by name. To do so would be considered the deepest insult."

To achieve a new and better name was the goal of many Pawnee males. Such a desire often prompted a man to attempt great deeds so that he may have a name-changing ritual, where his old name was discarded and a new, more respected name was bestowed. During such a ceremony, a Pawnee man's new name was proclaimed to everyone in the village. A man could later give his name to his son or daughter.

Names such as Chief Big Eagle, Big Sleight-of-Hand, Buffalo-Leader, and Coming-Downhill-Bringing-Trophies demonstrate the ideals utilized in Pawnee names.

The Life of Children

Children were considered gifts from the heavens. They were rarely disciplined and often spoiled—especially by grandparents. Babies were not allowed to cry, however, since such a noise might help an enemy locate the tribe. To prevent crying, the needs of the children were met immediately. If crying continued, a child's nose was held or water was poured in its nostrils until it stopped. The Pawnee did not believe in corporal punishment, and children were rarely hit or beaten. Instead, children were instructed to act properly by hearing stories of scary animals who might attack them if they did not cease their difficult behavior. As Mails writes:

Ponderous but entertaining lectures about responsibilities began at an early age, and the children had responded so well by the time they were ten or eleven that admonitions about discipline were no longer necessary. . . .

Parents encouraged the qualities of spirituality, pride, respect for elders, conformance to the tribal code of ethics and to the standard rules of etiquette. Every mother sang instructive lullabies which included lessons in morals and bravery. Tribal historians taught history, and other elders gave instructions in national loyalty.[44]

At play, Pawnee children practiced the roles they would assume as adults. Young boys had small bows and arrows with which they hunted rabbits and birds. From the age of ten, they went on hunting expeditions together where they learned to track animals and imitate the cries of the wolves, coyotes, and owls that populated the prairies. While growing up, boys were expected to be daring, agile, and able to endure physical pain. And they were encouraged to learn survival skills by taking long walks without food or water, or by staying awake for days at a time.

Young girls led much more sheltered lives than their brothers. They were given dolls in cradleboards and small tepees where they could play house. When a girl reached the age of ten, she was no longer allowed to play with boys. Instead she was instructed by her mother in the skills necessary to cook, sew, bead, and garden.

By the time a girl was fifteen, she could manage a household, erect a tepee, carve bowls, and feed her brothers with produce from her own garden plot. Meanwhile, the older women in the lodge would instruct her in the ways of courtship, love, marriage, and birth. It was important for a Pawnee girl to become accomplished in life's skills, so that she would be worthy of the honor and respect the tribe traditionally bestowed upon women.

Back to Tirawa

Pawnee people often lived long, productive lives. Common diseases that killed white people were virtually unknown among the tribes before the nineteenth century. The Pawnee, however, were often at war with

A Pawnee boy might have several different names over the course of his lifetime, each reflecting an unusual dream or noteworthy deed.

neighboring tribes, especially the Sioux, and women as well as men were sometimes killed in raids and battles.

Upon death, a Pawnee person was shod with special burial moccasins and dressed in his or her finest ceremonial outfit. Sometimes the body was wrapped in a blanket or reed mat. A special platform was built high on a hill, so the deceased would be close to Tirawa, and the possessions of the person would be hung from the scaffolding. Sometimes a great warrior's horse would be killed to accompany the man on his journey in the next world.

Even after death, Pawnee people were long remembered by their relatives. Their great deeds and life accomplishments were discussed for decades around fire pits. These stories inspired the living to achieve prominence in their lifetimes so they too would be remembered. In this way the grand circle of life, from birth to death to legend, continued on its path in the Pawnee universe.

Chapter 5

Winning and Losing Power

The Pawnee followed a warrior tradition dating back centuries, and war was as much a part of life on the Great Plains as hunting and farming. Success in battle was the way a Pawnee man gained respect, achieved prosperity, and attained immortality in the legends of his tribe.

When the Pawnee left their ancestral home and moved to Nebraska, they clashed with many tribes along the way. After settling in Nebraska, the Pawnee were rapidly followed by the Ponca, Omaha, Oto, and others. The Pawnee attacked these tribes, and after fierce, drawn-out battles, finally defeated them. The victorious Pawnee allowed the defeated tribes to live on the edges of their territory. In exchange for taxes in the form of trade goods, the Pawnee offered limited protection to the Ponca, Omaha, and Oto.

Counting Coup

Pawnee warriors were fearless. Victory did not include slaughter of the enemy, however. Rather, they gained respect by humiliating their opponents. This was achieved through a custom that was common among the Pawnee, as well as other Native American tribes, called "counting coup," in which a warrior hit or landed a blow upon an enemy. This term was taken from French trappers, but the Pawnee called the practice *tat-i-ki*, or "I-at-him-strike."[45]

The Pawnee believed that great bravery was required for a warrior to count coup by coming into such close contact with his enemy. To aid in this practice, warriors often had special sacred coup sticks, clubs, lances, or other items. Or, as Mails writes, one Pawnee warrior scored a coup "when he simply ran up to a fallen enemy and jumped on him with both feet."[46]

Although coup could be taken without killing a man, it was necessary to have witnesses to such an act. If an enemy was already dead, from an arrow, for instance, a Pawnee warrior would drag him to a safe place so that his tribesmen could witness him counting coup later on. After the first

Enemies on the Plains

Many of the Native American tribes on the plains were in more or less constant states of warfare. In *Pawnee Hero Stories and Folk Tales*, George Bird Grinnell discusses the many enemies of the Pawnee:

"In the old days before the coming of the whites the Pawnees had no enemies near at hand. They had conquered all surrounding nations, and claimed and held the country from the Missouri River to the Rocky Mountains, and from the Niobrara, south to the Arkansas River or to the Canadian. When they wished to go to war, they were forced to journey either to the Rocky Mountains to fight the Utes, or up the Missouri to attack the Crows, or down into Mexico to plunder the Spaniards, or into Texas to steal horses from the Comanches, the Wichitas and other southern tribes. Then the war parties were great bodies—sometimes one thousand men—and all on foot. Afterward, as settlements approached them and other tribes were driven into their country, and the different Pawnee bands were crowded together, their campaigns diminished in importance, the war parties became smaller and smaller, until at last only half a dozen men would start out, and sometimes a single individual would go off by himself to steal horses.

The Pawnee . . . had no friends upon the prairies save those whom they had conquered and held by fear. Foes swarmed about them. To the north were the different bands of the Dakotas and the Crows; to the west the Utes, with the Arapahoes, the Kiowas and the Cheyennes; and to the south the Comanches, Cheyennes, Kiowas, Kansas, Osages, and their relations the Wichitas. . . . As a result of this universal hostility, the Pawnees were constantly being attacked, and were constantly losing men, women, and children."

coup was taken, two more warriors could also strike the enemy, saying the words that translate to "now-it is-on top-lying."[47] Pawnee warriors also cut the hair and scalp off their enemies as proof of counting coup. Mails explains the value of coup:

The proudest day in the life of any young warrior occurred when he counted his first coup. And, every one that followed thereafter established a chain of indelible accomplishments. At dances and ceremonies he was expected to join the other warriors in recounting each coup which had been leveled in tribal defense; while others, particularly the young boys, listened wide-eyed, spellbound, and turning green with envy.[48]

By choosing honor over mass killing, Pawnee warriors could earn the respect of their enemies and remain alive to fight another day. As Grinnell writes: "It was more glorious for a war party to kill a single enemy without receiving a wound, than to kill a dozen, if thereby they lost a man."[49]

Ways of War

In addition to counting coup, victorious Pawnee warriors also captured trophies such as scalps, weapons, sacred medicine bundles, and horses from a vanquished foe. Horses were particularly valuable, and Pawnee legend states that the first horses obtained by the tribe were captured from a Cheyenne village in the distant past. According to the official website of the Pawnee Nation:

The Pawnees were well known for their ability to raid neighboring tribes and acquire their horses. They set out on foot and brought back hundreds of horses, especially from the tribes to the

War with other tribes was a way of life for the Pawnee. Here, they engage Sioux warriors.

south and southwest. Horses gave the Pawnees the mobility that made them a name to be feared by their enemies.[50]

Horse theft was a major cause of conflict between the tribes. If a Pawnee was killed during such a raid, his relatives might petition a war chief to declare that retribution was necessary. At a victim's funeral, the war chief would announce that he was seeking volunteers for a war party. Younger men who desired to prove their bravery were the most eager volunteers.

Several hundred men or more might gather when a war party was assembled. War chiefs called the men to council and a feast was held. Women served platters of buffalo and dog meat. After the meal, dancing and singing filled the night as warriors beat on drums, shook rattles, and danced using the motions of a ritual battle. Tobacco offerings were made to the war spirits, and prayers were offered for a safe return of the warriors. Shamans were asked to peer into the future and predict the outcome of the raid.

Once the war party entered enemy territory, it might break up into five or six groups of thirty to forty men. When the war parties were met by a large number of enemy warriors, bows were drawn on both sides and arrows rained down on the assembled warriors from a distance. After the initial skirmish, the men moved in for close combat, wielding ball-headed war clubs. Acts of bravery were highly valued on the battlefield as men attempted to count coup.

In some cases the raiders sneaked up on people working in fields or hunting and either killed and scalped them or took them

prisoner. When the war parties returned to their villages, they let out special whoops or cries to let people know if they had been successful or not. Sometimes deception and tricks were used to surprise the enemy. In *Pawnee Indians,* George E. Hyde describes one such event in which enemy forces dressed their horses in buffalo skins to attack a Skidi Pawnee village in 1771:

Hiding their main force behind [a] ridge, the [attackers] sent forward a decoy party to draw the Skidis into a trap. The warriors of the decoy party lay down on their horses' backs, covering themselves with hairy buffalo robes; and as day dawned they rode over the ridge slowly in single file and moved down toward the river, having the appearance from a distance of a band of buffalo coming down to the stream to drink. These warriors started from the east end of the ridge, crossed the open valley, and vanished among the thickets along the river bank; but the watchers in the Skidi villages had seen them; and the cry *Taraha! Taraha!*—Buffalo! Buffalo!—rang out in the dawn. Mounting in haste, a large body of Skidi hunters came pouring from the villages, splashed across the river, and rode swiftly eastward down the narrow valley. Approaching the point where the buffalo had been seen, to their amazement they were suddenly charged by a large force of [the enemy], who burst out of the brush along the river bank and slammed into them; and at the same moment a still larger body of [the en-

Only village chiefs could conduct business with European traders and for that reason alcohol did not become a problem among the Pawnee as it did with so many other tribes.

emy] appeared on the ridge, cutting off their line of retreat up the valley. Here many of the Skidis died, bravely fighting against overwhelming numbers. Some of them broke through the [enemy lines], swam their horses across the river, and rushed back to the villages, to protect the women and children.[51]

Resisting Intrusive Cultures

Although the Pawnee often clashed with neighboring tribes, they had peaceful relations with many of the earliest Europeans to arrive in the region.

When French fur traders came to the area in the 1700s, the Pawnee allowed them to cross their lands in peace. In exchange for this generosity, the French showered the Pawnee with gifts such as metal cookware,

steel knives, bolts of cloth, and guns and ammunition. By the 1720s the Pawnee traded regularly with French explorers.

Relations with the Spanish did not follow this pattern. The Spanish saw the Pawnee and other Native Americans as a source of slaves for their lucrative slave trade. Spanish soldiers kidnapped Native Americans and shipped them to sugar plantations in the Caribbean and elsewhere. By 1724 the situation was so bad that the Pawnee offered to trade thousands of beaver, buffalo, and otter hides to the French for a steady supply of firearms so they could defend themselves against slave traders.

Slavery was but one destructive force brought to the plains by the Europeans. Another was alcohol. At first, the Indians believed that alcohol had magical powers that could inspire visionary dreams. But alcohol had devastating effects on Native Americans. Their bodies could not tolerate the effects of intoxication, and addiction grew in most Native American populations.

The Pawnee, however, did not fall under the spell of alcohol. As White explains: "The Pawnees . . . remained a remarkably temperate people, and their abstinence was widely remarked upon on the plains. The Pawnees' refusal to accept liquor explains in large part their ability to avoid [loss of control over trade]."[52] The Pawnee were able to resist the temptations of alcohol because of the strong controls that chiefs had over com-

merce. No European trader could exchange goods with any Pawnee tribe member without first going through the village chiefs, and trades were always conducted in the chief's lodge. Those who resisted would find themselves facing village police officers who beat, whipped, or even killed traders who did not obey tradition.

The chief's job was made easier by the Pawnee preference for their own handiwork over many European trade goods. They traded with the Europeans when it most suited their purposes. While guns were effective weapons in war, rifles of the late eighteenth century were cumbersome in-

The Pawnee generally had little interest in the goods Europeans offered for trade since many were impractical or of poor quality.

struments that were hard to aim and even more difficult to reload on horseback. On the other hand, a bow-wielding warrior could rapidly fire up to five arrows in less than thirty seconds. In addition, a buffalo shot with a bullet often escaped and ran a long distance before dying. An arrow shot by a skilled hunter, however, rarely failed to bring the animal down.

Other trade goods held even less interest for the Pawnee. While they appreciated metal pots and knives, these items lasted for many years and did not often need to be replaced. And the shoddy factory-made clothing offered by traders was significantly inferior to the handmade buffalo and deerskin clothing of the Pawnee.

One Pawnee priest, quoted by White, summed up the attitude of traders. He said that they "come into our country to trade with us, and to give us all sorts of useless trash and poisoned drink for our best property . . . and to enrich [themselves] with our poverty."[53]

Disrupted Lives

As more Europeans drifted into the area, it became clear that the Pawnee would not be able to maintain strict control over their lands. Although they resisted pressures from the fur traders, other natives in the region did not. As the demand for furs increased by the 1820s, neighboring tribes began trespassing onto Pawnee lands to trap beaver, otter, elk, and deer; and the populations of many important game animals were nearly wiped out.

While this was a serious problem, nothing destroyed the Pawnee way of life faster than the introduction of European diseases, to which the tribes had no natural resistance. Smallpox and measles epidemics first hit the Pawnee villages in the 1750s, and smallpox returned again in the 1790s. At least one-third to one-half of the thirty-five thousand villagers died from these diseases.

After these epidemics had run their course, the Pawnee population grew again between 1800 and 1830. In 1823 a German duke, Paul Wilhelm, visited the Pawnee and reported that the chief had told him "the Pawnee nation counted as many heads as the stars in the sky, so that they could not be counted."[54] Unfortunately the smallpox epidemic of 1831 killed about half of the surviving Pawnee population in a matter of weeks. But even after these disasters, about ten thousand natives remained. In 1838 yet another smallpox epidemic killed about a quarter of the population, and by 1840 a little over six thousand Pawnee remained alive.

Disease weakened the tribes in many ways. In addition to the great grief caused by the deaths of loved ones, the epidemics caused the Pawnee to lose faith in their priests, doctors, and chiefs, who proved powerless to stop the ongoing disasters. At the same time, skilled farmers, craft workers, warriors, and others died before teaching their ancient skills to the next generation.

Signing Away the Land

The weakened Pawnee quickly began to lose control over their lands as competing tribes were forced westward by the rapidly expanding white population of the United States. In 1832, for instance, the Delaware tribe was pushed off its lands east of the Mississippi River. In response, the U.S. government granted the Delaware a large piece of territory directly in the center of the Pawnee buffalo hunting grounds in northwest Kansas. When the Pawnee discovered this new tribe on their land, they attacked them. In retaliation, the Delaware raided and set fire to a Pawnee village while its people were away on a hunt. This incident took place the year after the smallpox epidemic had killed half the tribe.

When Federal officials saw the weakened condition of the Pawnee they immediately took advantage of the situation by persuading tribal leaders to sign their lands over to the government and move to the Loup Fork Reservation in Nebraska. According to Hyde:

[A] treaty commission was sent to the Grand Pawnee village on the Platte, where the chiefs were quickly talked into signing away all the vast Pawnee territory south of the Platte.

The Pawnee chiefs seemed to believe that in signing this treaty, October 9, 1833, they were merely giving the Delaware and other immigrant tribes permission to hunt on their lands. They do not appear to have comprehended the government's true purpose, which was to obtain the Pawnee lands and then to attempt to end the ancient practice of wandering in the plains and to induce the Pawnees to settle down on Loup Fork, to give up hunting and roving, and to learn to live by agricul-

ture alone. The treaty therefore provided that whenever the tribe exhibited an honest purpose to abandon hunting and war and settle on the Loup Fork, the government was to send farmers to teach the Indians the white man's method of agriculture. Blacksmiths and schoolteachers were also to be provided, as well as a grist mill and agricultural implements. As the Pawnees had not the slightest intention of giving up hunting, all that they received for the vast tract of land ceded was $1,600 in goods.[55]

Government agents had little understanding of how this treaty would affect the tribe. The Pawnee could not even consider giving up the semiannual buffalo hunt, since the animals were much more than a food source for the Pawnee. As White writes: "[The] buffalo was a sacred animal; its meat, dedicated to the ceremonies by the hunters, in a sense fueled the whole Pawnee world. If they did not hunt buffalo, they could not offer meat at the ceremonies; if the meat was not offered, then *tirawahut* would be offended, crops would fail, and the Pawnees would suffer even more."[56]

The hopes of the Pawnee to continue hunting buffalo, however, meant little to the government. The United States was expanding at an incredibly rapid rate, and its people were obsessed with the region west of the Mississippi River. In 1842 the first wagon train of settlers crossed the Great Plains, and their numbers increased every year. When gold was discovered in California in 1848, an onslaught of pioneers invaded Pawnee territory,

The California Gold Rush of the 1840s brought pioneers streaming across the plains. Their presence drove away the buffalo, a primary source of food and clothing for the Pawnee.

heading west on the Oregon Trail, which followed the Platte River through Nebraska.

This encroaching population frightened off the buffalo, who not only avoided pioneers in settlements, but also stayed far away from the rapidly growing number of pioneer trails that crossed the area. According to White:

> By the mid-1840s the Pawnees were making numerous and direct complaints about the dearth of buffalo along the Platte and fixed responsibility on the Americans. In the 1840s Old Soldier, a Skidi, complained in council, "For a long time . . . the buffalos were plenty on the Platte. But now the whites have gone before us and will scare all the buffalo away." The next year a chief of the Grands rejected the usual presents paid by travelers for passage across Pawnee lands on the grounds that they did not compensate for the damage the

migrants did to the herds. The Pawnees denied that the whites had the right to pass through their country and imperil their whole economy.[57]

The Final Blow

The Pawnee had few allies to turn to, and their bitter enemies, the Sioux, were emboldened by their weakness. The Sioux had been attacking Pawnee villages and stealing their caches of food as early as 1820. In the summer of 1841, five hundred Sioux attacked a Skidi village and killed hundreds of people already weakened by epidemics. Similar attacks occurred almost annually. Women were killed by the Sioux in their farm fields, and hunters were slaughtered on the buffalo trail. These attacks aggravated all the other disasters befalling the Pawnee, as White explains:

> For a nation whose cultural ideal was peace and security, this endless warfare,

disease, death, and starvation had to have cultural consequences, which in turn influenced further Pawnee adjustments to the changes taking place around them. People were dying, but so too were basic elements of a cultural order. Because of the special mechanisms for communicating sacred knowledge, increasing death rates deprived the Pawnees of knowledge itself and the hierarchy it controlled. Sacred knowledge could only be legitimately acquired from a priest or chief in exchange for the proper gifts. Thus when a priest died before communicating all his wisdom, the knowledge died with him.[58]

Meanwhile government agents were pressuring the Pawnee to move onto tracts of land called reservations that were set apart by the federal government as places where the tribes could live. And instead of helping the Pawnee, who had never actively waged war against American civilians or soldiers, the government tried to stop attacks by Sioux by giving them weapons as peace offerings. Pawnee historians explain the damage caused by actions such as these:

Although the Pawnees never waged open war against the U.S. Government and were classified as a "friendly nation," extra privileges were not gained. The government felt the need to placate warring tribes with gifts, which sometimes consisted of rifles to hunt buffalo. These rifles were in turn used against other tribes, including the Pawnees, who were not so fortunately armed.[59]

Because of poor treatment by the U.S. government and ongoing warfare with the Sioux, the Pawnee population dwindled to just one thousand by 1900.

Pawnee Scouts

In the 1860s, while the U.S. military was busy fighting the Civil War, Sioux warriors killed hundreds of white settlers crossing the Great Plains. After the war, government attempts to control the Sioux failed miserably. In 1867, to win the war of the plains, the United States enlisted about two hundred Pawnee men as army scouts. The Pawnee were quick to join, eager to seek revenge on the Sioux, who had mercilessly attacked their people for decades.

The Pawnee scouts served under Major Frank North in what was called "the Sioux Campaign." North was such a respected leader that he was named Pani Leshar, or "Pawnee Chief," by the scouts. When the government wanted to build the transcontinental railroad several years later, the Pawnee were once again hired, this time to protect the railroad workers, who were under attack from Sioux, Cheyenne, and Arapaho warriors. Ironically, the trains brought thousands of settlers to the Great Plains, which soon forced the Pawnee from their ancestral homeland.

Although the Pawnee hoped that they would be given special consideration by the government for their efforts, they were treated no differently than any other tribe. Within a decade the Pawnee would be forced to give up their territory and move to a reservation in Oklahoma.

In 1859, weakened by hunger and disease, most Pawnee villagers moved to a reservation on the Loup River near present-day Genoa, Nebraska. Here they found no peace, as the Sioux continued their relentless raids. Many desperate Pawnee warriors joined the U.S. Army, acting as scouts in the government's battle against the Sioux in the 1860s and 1870s.

The final blow to Pawnee sovereignty occured during the annual buffalo hunt in 1873. Over a thousand Sioux warriors slaughtered hundreds of Pawnee hunters at a site that became known as Massacre Canyon near present-day Trenton, Nebraska. The loss of so many skilled hunters made it impossible for the Pawnee to support themselves. By 1875 there were fewer than twenty-five hundred Pawnee— less than 10 percent of the population that had lived in the region only fifty years earlier.

In 1876 the shrinking tribe of Pawnee was forced by the U.S. government to cede its Loup Fork reservation, which encompassed the tribe's ancestral hunting grounds. After surrendering their lands, the tribe was ordered to move to Oklahoma, where survival in the harsh, unfamiliar land would become an unrelenting challenge. By 1900 only a thousand members of the once-great Pawnee Nation were left alive.

Chapter 6

Life in the United States

By the 1880s, the buffalo were all but extinct on the Great Plains. Hundreds of white settlers were arriving every day, and the once wild grasslands were fenced off with miles of barbed wire. The native prairie was being plowed under by farmers to make way for wheat, alfalfa, oats, and other nonnative species. A way of life that had existed for the Native American tribes for hundreds of years had come to an end.

Where the Pawnee had once lived, steam-driven tractors pulled huge mechanical plows, reapers, threshers, and combines. The clean air of the prairies gave way to smoke-belching marvels of the machine age. Towns like Topeka, Kansas, and Omaha, Nebraska, had grown into major cities. They boasted such luxuries as electric lights, telephones, trolley cars, and paved streets.

As for the Pawnee, they unwillingly signed away portions of their lands to the U.S. government in 1833, 1848, 1857, and 1872. In 1875 they were forced to leave their homelands and resettle on a piece of territory known as the Pawnee Indian Agency, about forty miles west of Tulsa, Oklahoma.

The Pawnee made their final move to Oklahoma in three different groups, pulling their belongings in wagons supplied

By the 1880s, hundreds of settlers were pouring across the Great Plains and ending the Pawnee way of life forever.

A Pawnee chief negotiates with U.S. Army officials.

by the government. Once they arrived at the reservation, they set up three earth-lodge villages. One was built along the Arkansas River near Ralston, and two were constructed near the present-day town of Pawnee. Before five years had passed, however, more than eight hundred Pawnee died from disease.

Federal Acts and Allotments

While the Pawnee dealt with the sick and the dying in their traditional manner, government agents began drawing up new rules for the survivors. In the eyes of white inhabitants of the Great Plains, the Pawnee and other tribes simply stood in the way of progress. People in government wanted to force the tribe members to join in, or assimilate, into American culture.

In the late nineteenth century, the U.S. Congress enacted a series of laws designed to turn what were called "wild Indians" into average American farmers. In 1887 Congress passed the Dawes General Allotment Act, which would grant individual parcels of land on reservations to Native American men. It was believed that if each man farmed his own private plot of land, he could make a profit, support his family, and join white society. Author Kent Carter describes the thinking behind the Dawes Act:

It became almost an article of faith with the reformers that private ownership of property was one of the most powerful tools that could be used to bring about assimilation. They therefore set out to destroy the tribal governments and their system of communal ownership and give each Indian his . . . own piece of land. . . . They were convinced that such a policy would force the Indians to become more like the industrious white farmers who were rolling over them like a tidal wave. Powerful economic interests supported the policy because it would open surplus [federal] land to non-Indians.[60]

The Dawes General Allotment Act ignored several important facts of life among the Pawnee and other tribes. The Pawnee believed that all their territory, possessions, and even children belonged to the entire community; owning an individual piece of property was a foreign concept. More important, women were the farmers in Pawnee communities, so granting agricultural land to men was destined to fail.

After the General Allotment Act became law, the government worked in other ways to destroy tribal unity. In 1898 a law was passed known as the Curtis Act, named after Congressman Charles A. Curtis, who was one-eighth Kansa Indian. The Curtis Act outlawed tribal governments and put all Na-

The Dawes General Allotment Act

In 1887 a group of eastern reformers and western land speculators pushed a law through Congress called the Dawes General Allotment Act, named after Massachusetts senator Henry L. Dawes, who sponsored the bill. The law, also known as the Allotment Act, broke up the communal land of the reservations into 160-acre plots to be assigned to individual Native Americans. Unscrupulous Indian agents signed up dogs and dead people to reservation rolls to obtain extra grants of the 160-acre allotments.

According to the Allotment Act, any acreage left over after each Native American received 160 acres could be sold to white people. The reformers meant to destroy the group-oriented Native American culture and replace it with independent, land-owning capitalism.

In 1887, before the passage of the Allotment Act, Indian nations still held 138 million acres of land in the United States. By 1934, when the Allotment Act ended, 95 million of those acres had been lost or sold to whites. A large part of the remainder was under lease to whites. These developments occurred because many Native Americans were unable to adapt to farming and because much of the land was unsuitable to agriculture. More than ninety thousand Native Americans were left landless.

Beginning in 1887, the federal government required Indian children to attend school where they were taught how to live in white society.

tive Americans under the rule of federal law. The Curtis Act also gave authority to the secretary of the interior to sell Native American lands without notifying the tribes. These new government mandates nearly destroyed what was left of the Pawnee tribe. According to author Carl N. Tyson:

> Although the stronger tribes . . . were able to fight the government's high-handed methods, the Pawnee and other smaller groups were swept away by the process which the whites called "assimilation" or "Americanization." With the passage of the Curtis Act, the Pawnee once again descended to a place of darkness. Declared leaderless

by the government, made rootless by the Dawes Commission, and set adrift in a sea of whites by the creation of the state of Oklahoma in 1907, the Pawnee began to search for a light that would lead them from the hole. Their search was difficult and the wait was long.[61]

Indian Schools

After the passage of the Dawes Act, federal Indian agents began forcibly removing Native American children from their homes and sending them to schools to learn how to live like white people. The institutions were similar to reform schools, and children were forced to cut their hair, dress in

American-style clothing, and take American names, whereby a boy named Otter Tail, for example, might be called James. Terms lasted three years during which time students were not allowed to leave the premises. In addition, the children were forbidden to speak their native languages under threat of severe beatings.

Children of the Pawnee tribe were sent to the Pawnee Industrial School, on the Oklahoma reservation, and to "Indian schools" as far away as Pennsylvania and New Jersey. One such school was built close to the former Pawnee homeland near Genoa, Nebraska. The website maintained by the city describes the school:

On February 20, 1884, with an enrollment of 74 students, the U.S. Indian School at Genoa was started. The school began with one building on 320 acres and grew to have more than thirty buildings on 640 acres. The school was in operation for fifty years and became one of the largest of the Federal Boarding Schools. In 1932, the peak enrollment was nearly 600 students.

The school stressed assimilation into white society with a combination of manual training and basic education. The students spent half a day learning a trade and the other half learning reading, writing and math. The school closed in 1934. The students went back to their reservations, attended other boarding schools or went on to college.[62]

Slipping into Obscurity

With the children gone and the elders suffering from poverty and disease, little changed on the Pawnee reservation for the first three decades of the twentieth century. As Tyson writes: "From 1900 to 1934, the Pawnee appeared to slip into obscurity. Although individuals continued to join together for ceremonies . . . the tribe did not function. There was no tribe, only people."[63]

In the 1930s, the federal government sought to rectify some of the injustices that had been committed against the Pawnee and other tribes. In 1934 Congress passed the Indian Reorganization Act, which altered the way the federal government dealt with tribes. The act repealed provisions in the Dawes General Allotment Act and reinstated tribal governments, with leaders elected by tribe members. In addition, a scholarship fund was set up along with a program to give college loans to qualified Native American students. Two years later Congress set up the Indian Arts and Crafts Board to help native people sell their craftwork.

Unfortunately, the Pawnee were barely affected by the Reorganization Act since they had lost their land after the Curtis Act was instituted, as Tyson explains:

The excess lands of the reservation had been repossessed by the government after the destruction of the tribe, and the Secretary of Interior had ceded some of the lands to whites. Therefore, the tribal government was unable actively to run the business of the Pawnee. Without ownership of tribal lands, there was no business.[64]

Baseball Great Moses YellowHorse

Government-run Indian schools were managed more like prisons than institutions for learning. The only opportunity for students to run free came during sports activities. As such, several Native Americans who attended Indian schools became renowned professional athletes, including Moses YellowHorse, a Pawnee native who was a pitcher for the Pittsburgh Pirates. YellowHorse threw for the Pirates in 1921 and 1922 and was the only full-blooded Native American to ever play for a major league baseball team. Today his glove is on display at the Baseball Hall of Fame in Cooperstown, New York.

Despite their landless status, the Pawnee Nation adopted its own constitution in 1938, looking forward to the day when the tribe would once again own community land.

Regaining the Land

With the reformation of the tribal government, the Pawnee began a twenty-year-long series of legal battles in order to regain their lands. Finally, in 1957 the Department of the Interior gave the Pawnee the right to occupy several hundred acres of land surrounding the old Pawnee Industrial School. The lands, however, would still belong to the government.

This small step was the beginning of reparations to the Pawnee. The government had broken every treaty it had ever signed with any Native American tribe—including the Pawnee, and there was a growing movement in the 1960s to compensate them for this injustice. As Tyson writes:

According to the various treaties between the United States and the Pawnee, the tribe had been promised annuities [annual payments] . . . for lands in Nebraska. In the summer of 1964, the government paid the tribe a large sum for lands which had been sold in the 19th century. The Pawnee had been promised that the tracts would be auctioned for $1.25 an acre but the government's surveyors said land inspectors had sold much of the territory for as little as twenty-five cents an acre.[65]

With the funds released for Nebraska territory sold long ago, the Pawnee fought in court to regain title to their reservation in Oklahoma. After nine more years of legal battles, on October 2, 1968, Congress finally returned the lands to the tribe.

While the Pawnee celebrated their long-awaited victory, regaining the reservation did not immediately solve the problems the tribe was facing, as Tyson explains:

The return of the reserve to the tribe in 1968 did not cause immediate prosperity among the Pawnee or the creation of a viable government. Although plans were laid for tribal projects which would provide economic assistance to members and which would ease unemployment which averaged from sixty to seventy-five per cent, little was accomplished.[66]

The Modern Era

Fortunes of the tribe began to improve in 1975 when Thomas Chapman Jr., a strong tribal leader—and former U.S. Marine—took over as chief executive officer of the Pawnee tribe. Chapman helped the tribe to regain almost a hundred more acres that had been forfeited in the nineteenth century. He also drew on the talents of Pawnee accountants, businesspeople, and lawyers to take advantage of government grants and programs that were designed to help Native Americans.

Most important, Chapman instituted the Pawnee Heritage Program. According to Tyson:

This was designed to promote the reestablishment of the Pawnee language and culture among the remaining members of the tribe, and to provide opportunities to these members to achieve economic independence. [The] program consists of six projects, each with a specific goal: Heritage House, a facility which . . . [provides] a center for the collection and preservation of artifacts and data concerning the history of the Pawnee; Elders Council Center, to serve the elderly members of the tribe; Youth Council Center, to serve the young; Job Opportunity Office, to provide a center for employment information. . . . Tribal Industrial Park Authority, to facilitate the creation of an industrial park on the tribal lands. . . . And Tribal Finance Office, to give guidance and assistance to tribal members in companies locating in the industrial park.[67]

Although some of Chapman's initiatives were more successful than others, by focusing on culture and business, his policies helped turn the tribe's fortunes in a positive direction. Over the years his programs have evolved to fit the changing needs of the Pawnee community.

In 1982 the Pawnee constitution was amended to reflect the traditional form of Pawnee governance. Instead of having a single person act as president of the Pawnee Nation, the constitution allows for eight chiefs to serve on the governing body known as the Nasharo Council. In addition, the Pawnee government utilizes an eight-member business council, along with committees that oversee education, the elderly, and tribal health.

Among such programs are the Health and Community Services Department, which helps Pawnee people deal with mental health problems such as depression and suicide. The Substance Abuse Program helps those with alcohol and drug problems. The Elderly Feeding Program brings meals to older people who can no longer cook for themselves. The Indian Children Welfare Program provides counseling, shelter, and educational services to young people trapped in poverty. And the After School Program provides a center where, according to the Pawnee Nation website, "children can relax and release energy while they play both indoor and outdoor games, do arts and crafts, read, and participate in planned centers. Children are provided with a nutritious snack, tutoring, and homework help. They are also able to celebrate their pride and cultural awareness."[68]

Because of such programs, Pawnee children today have more opportunities than at any time in recent history. Local schools

Today, the Pawnee are working to reclaim their heritage and to educate their children and the world about the history and culture of their people.

The Pawnee Flag

The Pawnee Nation has its own flag, adopted in 1977, specifically designed to reflect the history and culture of the tribe. The flag is described by Don Healy on the "Flag of the Pawnee" website:

"This long association with the United States is reflected in the flag of the Pawnee Nation of Oklahoma today. . . . Their flag is blue and bears a small representation of a U.S. flag in the upper part of the flag. . . . This is faced by a red wolf's head, since the Indians of the Plains referred to the Pawnee as 'wolves' for their cunning and courage. This term translated into Pawnee as 'Men of Men'.

At the top and bottom of the flag are three narrow stripes, blue at the outermost, then white and finally red. . . . Below the wolf's head are a crossed tomahawk and peace pipe or calumet, also in red. The two de-

A representation of the flag of the Pawnee Nation.

vices represent peace and war. Finally, below the tomahawk and calumet are seven white arrowheads representing the seven wars in which the Pawnee have fought in the service of the United States—the Indian Wars, the Spanish-American War, both World Wars, Korea, Vietnam, and the Gulf War.

As an entity, the flag means 'Pawnee Indians, in peace and war, always courageous and always loyal to America.'. . .

The main flag of the Pawnee flown in the Tribal Headquarters in Pawnee, [Oklahoma,] is to be mounted on an oldtime Pawnee lance bearing a genuine flint spearhead. The shaft of the lance has a special strip of buckskin bearing intricate beadwork designs down the length of the staff. Attached to the spearhead at the top are four primary eagle feathers. . . .

The four feathers at top represent the four bands of the Pawnee—the Chauee, the Kitkahaki, Petahurat and Skedee. . . .

Recently, the Pawnee Nation modified the flag . . . to reflect participation in 'Operation Desert Storm.' The seventh arrowhead now appears in the row. . . . Previously the flag bore only six arrowheads."

have begun teaching Pawnee culture and history. Those interested in learning the Pawnee language meet twice a week for six-week semesters, and students listen to elders speak and also learn to write the language. In addition, government programs provide scholarships to any Pawnee interested in attending college or vocational school.

Celebrating the Past and the Future

Over the years many Pawnee have taken advantage of various educational opportunities and have become doctors, lawyers, and successful businesspeople. The Pawnee warrior tradition continues to remain a strong source of pride as Pawnee soldiers have served in World Wars I and II, the Korean War, the Vietnam War, and the Gulf War.

That pride is seen in the yearly Fourth of July Pawnee Indian Homecoming, a powwow established in 1946 by returning World War II veterans. The event is described on the Pawnee Nation website:

The Pawnee Indian Veterans Organization was organized immediately following the 1946 Homecoming and Powwow which was held to honor the returning servicemen and women from the battlefields of World War II and to remember those who made the supreme sacrifice. That initial Homecoming was organized by the Pawnee Indian Veterans of World War I. Billed as the Largest FREE Indian Powwow

in the World, the annual Pawnee Indian Homecoming and Powwow celebrates its 55th birthday in 2001. . . . The mile-long Homecoming parade through downtown Pawnee is another spectacle and includes participation of the whole community. Added attractions include the 1-mile Hawk Chief Run, named in honor of the famous Pawnee Scout and runner, the first man to run a sub 4 minute mile in 1876; and the annual Moses YellowHorse Co-ed Softball Tournament, named in honor of the American Indian Hall of Fame and Pittsburgh Pirate Pitcher, the only full-blood American Indian to play major league baseball. The annual Homecoming and Powwow is held the first weekend in July and generally includes Pawnee's huge 4th of July celebration.[69]

The annual powwow is a source of Pawnee pride and attracts hundreds of tourists who come to observe the tribe's cultural heritage. Although the tribal membership plunged from 35,000 in 1800 to less than 600 in 1900, there are over 2,500 Pawnee alive today. And the tribe has managed to retain the traditional ways of their ancestors while embracing the computer age to keep that heritage alive.

The state of the Pawnee tribe in the twenty-first century is described on their official website:

Pawnees can be found in all areas of the United States as well as foreign countries in many walks of life.

Pawnees take much pride in their ancestral heritage. They are noted in history for their tribal religion, rich in myth, symbolism and elaborate rites.[70]

From the time the Pawnee walked from Texas to Nebraska to become the most powerful tribe on the plains, their history and culture have been evolving. As modern society moves ahead with progress and promise, the Pawnee people continue to celebrate their revered ancient traditions in a world that has changed so much in so little time.

Notes

Chapter 1: Villages on the Plains

1. Matthew W. Stirling, "Indians of Our Western Plains," *National Geographic*, July 1944, p. 80.
2. Gene Weltfish, *The Lost Universe*. Lincoln: University of Nebraska Press, 1965, p. 265.
3. Stirling, "Indians of Our Western Plains," p. 80.
4. Weltfish, *The Lost Universe*, p. 14.
5. Weltfish, *The Lost Universe*, pp. 252–53.
6. Quoted in Weltfish, *The Lost Universe*, pp. 383–84.
7. Quoted in Weltfish, *The Lost Universe*, p. 384.
8. Quoted in Weltfish, *The Lost Universe*, p. 385.
9. Thomas E. Mails, *The Mystic Warriors of the Plains*. New York: Marlowe, 1995, p. 347.
10. George Bird Grinnell, *Pawnee Hero Stories and Folk Tales*. New York: Forest and Stream Publishing, 1889, pp. 269–70.
11. Weltfish, *The Lost Universe*, p. 6.

Chapter 2: The Circle of the Seasons

12. Weltfish, *The Lost Universe*, p. 103.
13. Quoted in Weltfish, *The Lost Universe*, p. 103.
14. Richard White, *The Roots of Dependency*. Lincoln: University of Nebraska Press, 1983, p. 159.
15. Weltfish, *The Lost Universe*, p. 138.
16. George Bird Grinnell, *Pawnee, Blackfoot and Cheyenne*. New York: Charles Scribner's Sons, 1961, pp. 17–18.
17. Weltfish, *The Lost Universe*, p. 174.
18. Stirling, "Indians of Our Western Plains," p. 97.
19. Quoted in Weltfish, *The Lost Universe*, p. 251.

Chapter 3: Spirits, Priests, and Ceremonies

20. Grinnell, *Pawnee, Blackfoot and Cheyenne*, pp. 39–40.
21. White, *The Roots of Dependency*, p. 155.
22. Weltfish, *The Lost Universe*, p. 64.
23. Weltfish, *The Lost Universe*, p. 82.
24. White, *The Roots of Dependency*, p. 172.
25. White, *The Roots of Dependency*, p. 173.
26. Preston Holder, *The Hoe and the Horse on the Plains*. Lincoln: University of Nebraska Press, 1970, p. 46.
27. White, *The Roots of Dependency*, p. 172.
28. Weltfish, *The Lost Universe*, p. 254.
29. Weltfish, *The Lost Universe*, p. 257.
30. Weltfish, *The Lost Universe*, pp. 259–60.
31. Maggie Debelius and Stephanie Lewis, *The Buffalo Hunters*. Alexandria, VA: Time-Life Books, 1993, p. 162.
32. Colin F. Taylor, *The Plains Indians*. London: Salamander Books, 1994, p. 68.

33. Stirling, "Indians of Our Western Plains," pp. 107–108.
34. Weltfish, *The Lost Universe*, pp. 63–64.

Chapter 4: Men, Women, and Families
35. White, *The Roots of Dependency*, p. 175.
36. Weltfish, *The Lost Universe*, p. 16.
37. Weltfish, *The Lost Universe*, p. 16.
38. Debelius and Lewis, *The Buffalo Hunters*, pp. 70–71.
39. Weltfish, *The Lost Universe*, p. 17.
40. Weltfish, *The Lost Universe*, p. 25.
41. Quoted in Weltfish, *The Lost Universe*, p. 21.
42. Weltfish, *The Lost Universe*, p. 105.
43. Mails, *The Mystic Warriors of the Plains*, p. 512.
44. Mails, *The Mystic Warriors of the Plains*, p. 514.

Chapter 5: Winning and Losing Power
45. Quoted in Weltfish, *The Lost Universe*, p. 478.
46. Mails, *The Mystic Warriors of the Plains*, p. 297.
47. Quoted in Weltfish, *The Lost Universe*, p. 478.
48. Mails, *The Mystic Warriors of the Plains*, p. 295.
49. Grinnell, *Pawnee Hero Stories and Folk Tales*, p. 304.
50. "History of Pawnee Nation," Pawnee Nation of Oklahoma, August 28, 2000. www.pawneenation.org/.
51. George E. Hyde, *Pawnee Indians*. Denver: University of Denver Press, 1951, p. 75.
52. White, *The Roots of Dependency*, p. 191.
53. Quoted in White, *The Roots of Dependency*, p. 191.
54. Quoted in White, *The Roots of Dependency*, p. 154.
55. Hyde, *Pawnee Indians*, pp. 135–36.
56. White, *The Roots of Dependency*, p. 206.
57. White, *The Roots of Dependency*, p. 170.
58. White, *The Roots of Dependency*, pp. 207–208.
59. "History of Pawnee Nation," Pawnee Nation of Oklahoma, August 28, 2000. www.pawneenation.org/.

Chapter 6: Life in the United States
60. Kent Carter, "Snakes and Scribes: The Dawes Commission and the Enrollment of the Creeks," *Prologue: Quarterly of the National Archives and Records Administration*, Spring 1997. http://merrimack.nara.gov/publications/prologue/carter1.html.
61. Carl N. Tyson, *The Pawnee People*. Phoenix: Indian Tribal Series, 1976, p. 93.
62. "Historical Facts: Genoa, Nebraska," Nebraska Public Power District, 1997. www.ci.genoa.ne.us/hist.htm.
63. Tyson, *The Pawnee People*, pp. 92, 94.
64. Tyson, *The Pawnee People*, p. 94.
65. Tyson, *The Pawnee People*, p. 96.
66. Tyson, *The Pawnee People*, pp. 96–97.
67. Tyson, *The Pawnee People*, pp. 99–100.
68. "After School Program," Pawnee Nation of Okalahoma, August 28, 2000 www.pawneenation.org/programs/aftrschprog.htm.
69. "Pawnee Associations," Pawnee Nation of Oklahoma, August 28, 2000. www.pawneenation.org/.
70. "History of Pawnee Nation," Pawnee Nation of Oklahoma, August 28, 2000. www.pawneenation.org/.

For Further Reading

Maggie Debelius and Stephanie Lewis, *The Buffalo Hunters*. Alexandria, VA: Time-Life Books, 1993. A colorful and informative book illustrated with photos, paintings, and maps about the various tribes, including the Pawnee, that once hunted buffalo on the Great Plains.

Elizabeth Hahn, *The Pawnee*. Vero Beach, FL: Rourke Publications, 1992. A short history of Pawnee art, warfare, culture, and hunting techniques.

Theresa Jensen Lacy, *The Pawnee*. New York: Chelsea House, 1996. Part of the Indians of North America series covering the culture, religion, and history of the Pawnee from ancient history to the twentieth century.

Thomas E. Mails, *The Mystic Warriors of the Plains*. New York: Marlowe, 1995. A thorough reading of the culture, arts, crafts, and religion of the Great Plains tribes. The author has written eleven books about Plains people, and this book was used by Kevin Costner as a resource text for the movie *Dances with Wolves*.

Arthur Myers, *The Pawnee*. New York: Franklin Watts, 1993. An easy-to-read book that explores Pawnee village life, religious ceremonies, and the near destruction of their ancient culture by the hands of white civilization.

Gene Weltfish, *The Lost Universe*. Lincoln: University of Nebraska Press, 1965. Beginning in 1928, the author studied myths, tales, and life experiences of elders to write about prereservation Pawnee life. Weltfish is an anthropologist fluent in the Pawnee language, and this book is one of the most complete ethnologies of the Pawnee ever written.

Works Consulted

Books and Periodicals

Benjamin Capps, *The Great Chiefs*. Alexandria, VA: Time-Life Books, 1975. A large, colorful book rich in details about nineteenth-century Native American Chiefs who faced the daunting task of leading their people into a new era.

George Bird Grinnell, *Pawnee, Blackfoot and Cheyenne*. New York: Charles Scribner's Sons, 1961. Writing in 1870, the author was one of the first white people to record sympathetic accounts of the Pawnee. This book relates details from the summer buffalo hunt that the author attended as well as hero stories and folktales told by village elders. Grinnell's writings form the basis for much of the modern understanding of the Pawnee before white civilization intruded.

——, *Pawnee Hero Stories and Folk Tales*. New York: Forest and Stream Publishing, 1889. In this book, Grinnell visits elders on a reservation and records their stories about supernatural beliefs and the Pawnee way of life before the coming of white settlers.

Preston Holder, *The Hoe and the Horse on the Plains*. Lincoln: University of Nebraska Press, 1970. A study of the cultural development of the Native American tribes on the Great Plains.

George E. Hyde, *Pawnee Indians*. Denver: University of Denver Press, 1951. A book that covers the minutiae of four hundred years of times, dates, and places of Pawnee battles against other tribes and white soldiers.

Peter Nabokov, ed., *Native American Testimony*. New York: Thomas Y. Crowell, 1978. This book is a moving anthology of Native American and white encounters as seen through native eyes from the time of the Pilgrims to the era of the reservations. The editor draws on speeches, letters, autobiographies, and government documents to paint a powerful and vivid picture of a culture under siege.

Matthew W. Stirling, "Indians of Our Western Plains," *National Geographic*, July 1944. An article about the tribes of the western

Great Plains including the Pawnee as well as the Comanche, Kiowa, Arapaho, and Cheyenne.

John R. Swanton, *Source Material on the History and Ethnology of the Caddo Indians*. Washington, DC: Bureau of American Ethnology, 1942. A book about the history and culture of the Caddo tribe, ancestors of the Pawnee.

Colin F. Taylor, *The Plains Indians*. London: Salamander Books, 1994. An oversize book with many illustrations and photos that explores the lives and history of the Plains tribes.

Carl N. Tyson, *The Pawnee People*. Phoenix: Indian Tribal Series, 1976. The story of the Pawnee and their historic relations with European and American settlers, written by an assistant professor of history at Oklahoma State University.

Richard White, *The Roots of Dependency*. Lincoln: University of Nebraska Press, 1983. The author insightfully combines anthropology, history, and ecology to shed light on Pawnee culture in their native territories before and after the arrival of American civilization.

Internet Sources

Kent Carter, "Snakes and Scribes: The Dawes Commission and the Enrollment of the Creeks," *Prologue: Quarterly of the National Archives and Records Administration,* Spring 1997. http://merrimack.nara.gov/publications/prologue/carter1.html. A detailed article by the regional administrator of the National Archives and Records Administration–Southwest Region in Fort Worth, Texas, about the Dawes Act and how it affected the Creek and other Native American tribes.

Don Healy, "Flag of the Pawnee." http://user.aol.com/donh523/navapage/pawn.htm. A website that has a picture and information about the official Pawnee flag.

"Historical Facts: Genoa, Nebraska," Nebraska Public Power District, 1997. www.ci.genoa.ne.us/hist.htm. A website that details the history of the small town built by Mormon settlers on the site of the ancient Pawnee homeland.

Pawnee Nation of Oklahoma, August 28, 2000. www.pawneenation.org/. The official website of the Pawnee Nation of Oklahoma with links to Pawnee history, events, and members directory.

Index

Picture Credits

Cover Photo: © R. W. Jones/Corbis
© Bettmann/Corbis, 75
© R. W. Jones/Corbis, 81
Library of Congress, 12, 29, 35, 49, 67, 71, 72, 74, 77
© David Muench/Corbis, 28
North Wind Picture Archives, 30, 32
Peter Newark's American Pictures, 13, 37, 50, 65, 68
Peter Newark's Western Americana, 58
Prints Old and Rare, 42
Martha Schierholz, 40
© Richard Hamilton Smith/Corbis, 26
Smithsonian Institution, 18, 20, 22, 44, 55, 61
Stock Montage, 15
Western History Collections, University of Oklahoma, 53, 57

About the Author

Stuart A. Kallen is the author of over more than 150 nonfiction books for children and young adults and has written extensively on the subjects of American and Native American history. In addition, Mr. Kallen has written award-winning children's videos and television scripts. In his spare time, Stuart A. Kallen is a singer/songwriter/guitarist in San Diego, California.